DO-IT-YOURSELF
Eye Movement Technique

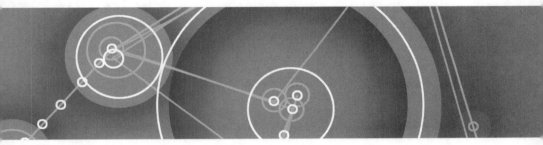

for Emotional Healing

Fred Friedberg, Ph.D.

Foreword by Matthew McKay, Ph.D.

New Harbinger Publications, Inc.

Publisher's Note

The do-it-yourself eye movement technique described in this book is provided for educational and informational purposes only. This technique is not intended to substitute for consultation or treatment by a health care professional. Please consult a physician, mental health professional, or other appropriate health care professional about the applicability of the technique for any symptoms or medical conditions you have.

This book is intended for the average person who functions pretty well already, but would like to reduce unwanted or undesirable levels of stress in his or her life. For such individuals, the do-it-yourself eye movement technique as described in this book can be beneficial and does not require professional assistance. The technique is not intended as a form of treatment for mental or emotional disorders.

As with any stress reduction technique, it is possible, though it occurs rarely, that certain individuals may experience an adverse reaction. Adverse reactions may take the form of distressing feelings, sensations, or memories. The standard relaxation exercises given in the book often may be used to successfully alleviate any distress. If the distress does not resolve, the individual should consult a family physician or mental health professional.

Distributed in the U.S.A. by Publishers Group West; in Canada by Raincoast Books; in Great Britain by Airlift Book Company, Ltd.; in South Africa by Real Books, Ltd.; in Australia by Boobook; and in New Zealand by Tandem Press.

Copyright © 2001 by Fred Friedberg
New Harbinger Publications, Inc.
5674 Shattuck Avenue
Oakland, CA 94609

Cover design and interior art by Lightbourne Images
Cover illustration by Bob Swingle
Edited by Sheila Freeman
Text design by Michele Waters

Library of Congress number: 01-132285
ISBN 1-57224-256-6 Paperback

Printed in the United States of America

New Harbinger Publications' Web site address: www.newharbinger.com

03   02   01

10   9   8   7   6   5   4   3   2   1

First printing

Contents

Foreword

In the past fifteen years there have been major advances and several new therapies for treating trauma and emotional pain. The most widely used, and best researched of these, are the eye movement techniques (EMT). Until this book, the extraordinary healing effects of EMT were provided only by therapists—a trained professional had to do it for you. Dr. Fred Friedberg has changed all that. For the first time, one of the most effective treatments ever developed for emotional pain has been restructured so you can do it yourself.

Before talking more about the unique contributions of Dr. Friedberg and this book, I want to back up a minute and tell you a bit of the history of EMT. A variant of EMT was first used to treat traumatized combat veterans. It was discovered that if they visualized a traumatic war scene, and then swept their eyes back and forth laterally, the scene would gradually become less and less disturbing. Many research studies confirmed this strong effect. A large number of men who had struggled with post-traumatic stress disorder—some of them for years—showed dramatic improvement in levels of anxiety, anger, flashback symptoms, and a host of other trauma-related problems.

The technique definitely worked. But no one knew why. Initially, it was thought that eye movement techniques owed their effectiveness to the phenomenon of rapid eye movement (REM). When people dream, their eyes tend to move back and forth. Since dream content often reflects daily problems and emotional struggles, perhaps the REM phenomenon—and EMT as well—was the body's natural way of processing trauma.

It was a great theory, but turned out not to be true. EMT works just as well with sounds . . . and touch. For example, if you hear clicking sounds alternating back and forth from one ear to the other, that can also provide emotional relief. The same is true if you are touched alternately on one side of your body, and then the other. Clearly, EMT isn't just a visual phenomenon, and can't be explained as something that mimics REM sleep.

Another theory is that EMT is nothing more than exposure. The idea is that if you visualize disturbing scenes over and over, you gradually get used to them. You get inured to the pain. But that doesn't explain why EMT works to relieve emotional distress *independent* of traumatic imagery. You can get relief with no visualization whatsoever.

Newer theories focus on the common factor in all EMT treatments—alternating stimulation of opposite sides of your brain. Whether your eyes move back and forth, or you hear alternating clicks, or you tap one leg and then the other, you are sequentially stimulating first one, and then the other side of your brain. Something about this bilateral stimulation relieves emotional pain. Anxiety, anger, guilt, shame—almost any kind of emotional arousal—diminishes with EMT. We still don't really know why; we just know it works.

While traditional forms of EMT were usually directed at traumatic memories, Dr. Friedberg realized that the focus of the technique could be broadened to almost any kind of painful emotion. Instead of targeting disturbing images from the past, he used EMT to relieve emotional distress *in the present*. He concerned himself not with old trauma, but with how you are feeling right now.

Shifting from a trauma to an emotion focus was the first of two radical departures Dr. Friedberg has made. The second has been to simplify and streamline EMT so anyone can use it. In this book, you will learn to use either alternating tapping on your legs or lateral eye movements to relieve emotional pain. Both variations of EMT work well; both are easy to master.

Dr. Friedberg's self-help EMT is a huge milestone because it makes available to *everyone* a therapy that is among the most effective ever devised. The healing power of EMT is no longer a closely held secret of the mental health profession. Instead, it's a set of simple steps that you can learn and put to use in just a few hours. I'm not exaggerating when I say that if you can tell time, you can do Dr. Friedberg's self-help EMT.

For those who are thinking this is too good to be true, let me offer the following:

1. Several studies have confirmed that EMT relieves stress and anxiety symptoms.

2. Fred Friedberg has taught his self-help EMT to more that 200 patients, and 75 to 80 percent have reported significant positive effects.

3. A growing number of therapists (including myself) are now teaching Dr. Friedberg's self-help EMT to their patients—with similar outcomes in effectiveness.

It's not often that a really good new treatment comes along. And it's rarer still when such a treatment is "given away" so anyone can access and use it. For these reasons, I am very pleased to introduce *Do-It-Yourself Eye Movement Technique for Emotional Healing.* When you'll learn here could change your life.

—Matthew McKay, Ph.D.,
Coauthor of *The Relaxation & Stress Reduction Workbook* and *Self-Esteem*

CHAPTER 1

The Potential Promise of a New Technique

If you feel overwhelmed by stress and at the same time wonder how you will find a few precious minutes to unwind and de-stress, then you can benefit from a new and innovative technique called *eye movement technique* or *EMT*. The actual procedure involves a rapid, back and forth movement of the eyes or a tapping of the fingers. This technique can provide made-to-order solutions for seemingly uncontrollable stresses. EMT will rapidly reduce emotional stress and redirect thinking in a positive, rational, and optimistic way. The technique, discovered about ten years ago, can be learned easily by almost anyone. This book will show you how to use the technique for quick stress relief and problem resolution. (Caution: If you have a history of trauma or current symptoms of post-traumatic stress disorder [disturbing memories of past events, flashbacks, nightmares, and sleep problems, panicky feelings, and/or have constant fear and tension], or if you have symptoms such as hallucinations, serious mood swings or suicidal thoughts, do not attempt to treat yourself with EMT. Likewise, if you have been diagnosed with dissociative personality disorder (multiple personality), schizophrenia, bipolar disorder (manic depression), or borderline personality disorder, do not self-treat with EMT. Seek treatment from a qualified psychotherapist.)

Converting the Skeptics

Although I am convinced of the unique power of EMT to eradicate stress, family and friends viewed it with disbelief when I first presented it to them. A longtime psychologist friend, Doreen, was highly skeptical of it. We had many discussions about the technique as I was writing this book. When I described the unusual fingertapping and eye movements of EMT, she practically accused me of being a charlatan. She couldn't believe that such ordinary physical movements could produce new attitudes and solve problems. This led to a heated argument.

Then, several weeks after our dispute about EMT, Doreen confided to me that she was afraid to drive into busy intersections. This problem had started for her on a stormy evening. Doreen was first in line at a stoplight when the vehicle behind her bumped her car forward. No one was injured. But since the accident she had become very fearful at intersections, worrying that her car would roll into the busy cross street. At stoplights, the fear caused her to grasp the wheel tightly, put the car in park, and forcefully pump the brake. She also scrutinized the cross traffic, worrying that a car might run into her vehicle.

Now I had an opportunity to help her with this new technique, and perhaps convince her that it was a legitimate intervention rather than a glorified parlor trick. When I offered to treat her problem with EMT, she was as skeptical as ever, but agreed to try it.

Doreen experienced a high level of stress just thinking about a busy intersection. As she focused on this stress, I tapped her hands during the first round of EMT. She immediately felt dizzy and the fearful image intensified. This reaction sometimes occurs initially. In the second EMT series, I shifted to back and forth eye movements, which reminded her of the sweeping windshield wipers on the rainy night when the accident occurred. Once again her fear increased. (When an individual's stress level increases during EMT, it is often helpful to switch to another type of eye movement. This is explained in chapter 5.)

During the third EMT series, I waved my hand up and down as her eyes followed the hand motions. After only two up-and-down eye movements, the frightening image completely disappeared. Remarking "It's gone," Doreen felt her fear about busy intersections evaporate. Even more surprising, she became enthusiastic, rather than apprehensive, about her next encounter with the driving situation—a situation that had terrified her only minutes before.

A week after the EMT visit, Doreen called me about two experiences she's had driving into intersections during a heavy nighttime rainstorm. As she slowed down at the stoplight, she noticed that her hands were loosely holding the steering wheel rather than overgripping it. Her legs and feet were also relaxed and she did not pump the brake excessively. Doreen felt a twinge of fear when a car with a boat trailer turned the corner next to her vehicle, but this fear was appropriate to the situation: The boat did come very close to her car, yet her fear passed quickly. She did not need to use EMT on herself.

Prior to the EMT session, Doreen's driving fear was spreading beyond intersections to driving on major expressways. Now, since the EMT session, the driving phobia was completely gone. How can this apparent eradication of the problem be explained? In general, new therapies may succeed because people hope and expect that they will. But Doreen didn't feel at all optimistic or confident about EMT. She thought of it as a modern form of snake oil. Yet, the EMT virtually cured her problem.

Was EMT merely a type of distraction? Apparently not. Before the treatment, Doreen had often tried to focus away from her driving fears and think about other things. It didn't work. Although she didn't understand how or why the EMT worked, her experience with the technique convinced her that it was a legitimate form of treatment.

What really happened during Doreen's session? The EMT probably acted as a potent relaxation technique that reduced the targeted fear and triggered a rapid and spontaneous rethinking of the dangers of driving into an intersection. And the new thinking "stuck" with her. Six months later, the driving fear had not returned. This positive result could happen in cognitive behavioral therapy—the most effective treatment for phobias—but it takes four to six visits, not five minutes.

EMT for Marital Worries

I also found a very skeptical audience for EMT with Bill, a thirty-nine-year-old client of mine. He was worried sick that his newly employed wife would be drawn into an extramarital affair. Despite their stable fifteen-year marriage, he was preoccupied with this unfounded fear. In the therapy session, I asked Bill, "Do you want to be cured of this obsession?" He laughed, looked at me cynically, and replied, "I don't think this kind of problem can be cured." I explained EMT and then demonstrated the technique on him. Afterward, his first reaction was one of complete surprise: "I'm just not thinking about it. What happened? It's like the problem just disappeared." Two weeks later, the worry was very minimal and did not interfere with his daily routine. Because I had no further contact with him, I cannot say for certain that the intense worry about his wife never resurfaced. But I did teach him the technique for home use in case the worry flared up again. In my long experience treating anxiety problems, even a two-week break from constant worry is an impressive outcome.

Overcoming Speaking Fears with EMT

Fear of public speaking is another common stress problem that can be alleviated with EMT. Although Carolyn, a well-known educator, gave numerous professional and public talks, she experienced high levels of anxiety weeks before a major speech. Two public speaking courses helped her to prepare and organize her talks, but her speeches remained stilted and boring. She could not project the animated, entertaining style of her ordinary conversations. When I presented the possibility of applying EMT to her speaking fear, she was initially reluctant about trying such a strange procedure. Yet a five-minute EMT session reduced her speaking fear in stages: First, she noticed that her neck was much more relaxed while thinking about giving a talk; then she imagined she *could* present an effective speech; with more confidence finally, she just stopped worrying about her next presentation. At a teachers conference three weeks later, she delivered a talk with much more confidence and vitality. The feedback she received afterward confirmed that her presentation skills had improved.

How did the EMT help? The procedure acted as both a powerful and enduring relaxation technique that calmed her public speaking fears, and as a visualization technique that allowed her to imagine speaking in a more spontaneous, self-assured manner.

In situations similar to the above vignettes, I have seen dramatic changes using EMT with over two hundred of my clients. As a psychologist in practice for eighteen years, I have never encountered such a powerful technique. It is surprisingly quick and effective. Contrary to the usual assumptions about psychotherapy requiring several weeks, months, or even years to be effective, EMT can produce significant and lasting emotional changes within minutes.

Origins of EMT

EMT was developed in the early 1990s as a technique that could quickly reduce emotional distress in people with post-traumatic stress disorder and other difficult stress problems (Marquis 1991; Smyth 1994; Wolpe and Abrams 1991). Over three hundred individuals were successfully trained to use EMT to reduce high levels of stress without any reported adverse effects. One advantage of the technique: It was quite portable. It could be used in almost any situation to relieve moderate to high levels of distress.

Following these early developments, EMT has evolved along two distinctly different paths. One elaboration of the method is now called EMDR™, an acronym for "eye movement desensitization and reprocessing." EMDR™ adds to the original method of EMT a detailed eight-step model of treatment that is intended for licensed psychotherapists to learn and then use with their patients who have post-traumatic stress disorder and other forms of emotional stress. Published books on EMDR™ contain frequent and forceful admonitions against therapists (and certainly non-therapists) using the technique without specialized training. According to the definitive professional volume on EMDR™ principles and procedures (Shapiro

1995), "Only licensed mental health professionals . . . should use the procedures in this book" (ix). And ". . . [the use of EMDR™] demands that training be obtained from EMDR™-authorized instructors and training seminars." (371)

The use of EMDR™ by untrained persons may generate the risk of sudden, disturbing recollections of traumatic events. The untrained EMDR™ user presumably wouldn't know how to resolve potentially damaging emotional upheavals. Dr. Francine Shapiro, the originator of EMDR™, further warns that "the lack of adequate screening, preparation, or implementation of EMDR™ can have literally fatal consequences [such as suicide attempts]. . . ."(Shapiro 1995, p. 303). Despite these strong caveats and ominous predictions, I have found no scientific evidence of such dangers in EMDR™ applications. In addition, as a fully trained EMDR™ clinician with nearly a decade of experience using the technique, I have not seen adverse reactions in any of my patients.

Although some individuals may experience upsets during the course of EMDR™ or EMT, this is what you would expect in any form of psychotherapy. People may get upset when they talk or think about their problems, whether you are using EMDR™, EMT, or any other treatment. Upsets related to these techniques are no more difficult to manage and resolve than upsets that occur without them. So I do not endorse the notion that EMDR™ and EMT are associated with unique dangers and risks.

This book develops the EMT concept into a generally useful and accessible technique. Based on my treatment of over two hundred patients with EMT, I have standardized and simplified the procedure so that it can be used by almost anyone for stress-related problems. You do not have to be a psychotherapist. You do not need extensive training. And I do not assume that you must revive childhood memories to feel better. Rather than focusing on trauma-related problems, which are best handled by an experienced psychotherapist, my brand of EMT works well with almost any type of stress related to everyday living, relationship difficulties, job dissatisfaction, and even chronic medical conditions. Once you learn how to do EMT, I think you will agree with me that it's a powerful and long-lasting stress reduction technique.

A Preliminary Study of EMT

Although I am convinced of the benefits of EMT based on years of experience treating patients with the technique, I understand the need for scientific research to confirm my clinical experience. As a psychologist in private practice, I fund my own research and publish the results in psychological and medical journals. These research efforts provide some level of scientific recognition and credibility for the work that I do.

I recently completed a preliminary study of EMT in people with fibromyalgia, an illness that is difficult to diagnose and treat, both medically and psychologically. According to Dr. John Sarno, a medical expert on chronic pain and author of *The Mind-Body Prescription* (1998), fibromyalgia is a type of chronic pain syndrome that is unusually severe. People with fibromyalgia suffer with widespread bodily pain and persistent fatigue that may prevent them from working and may reduce their ability to do everyday activities. The limitations caused by the illness can trigger enormous stress and frustration.

No curative medical treatment is available for fibromyalgia and many physicians are openly skeptical of the condition. As a result, individuals with the illness may have great difficulty finding a physician who is willing to offer treatment, if only for medication-based symptom management. The absence of medical recognition adds to the already substantial burdens on these patients.

I reasoned that if EMT could be effective in highly stressed people with fibromyalgia, then it could be at least as helpful for the stresses of everyday life that we all endure. Six women with an average illness duration of 9.5 years volunteered for my study. Their ages ranged from thirty-seven to fifty-three, four were married, and four were working part-time. The formal study consisted of two forty-five-minute sessions of EMT one week apart and a follow-up evaluation three months later. Between sessions, subjects were instructed to use the EMT daily to reduce stress and heighten relaxation.

To verify that EMT produced actual physical relaxation during the sessions, I hooked up each participant to a thermal biofeedback machine. This device measures the skin temperature of the hand using a thermal sensor attached to the index finger. Thermal biofeedback is a well-established, objective method of measuring physiologic stress and relaxation.

A battery of pen-and-paper tests were also given at both the EMT sessions and the follow-up visit in order to assess daily functioning, levels of anxiety and depression, and fatigue severity. All participants reported that the illness had a major impact on their daily activities, and all experienced high levels of anxiety, depression, and fatigue. Study participants were highly motivated to try this new technique that might make them feel better. Of course, I was enthusiastic about EMT, and I didn't want to disappoint them.

The results of the EMT were impressive. Five out of the six participants showed substantial improvements. The pen-and-paper tests completed at session two showed these average changes for the six subjects: a 30 percent reduction in anxiety scores, a 29 percent reduction in depression scores, a 13 percent reduction in illness impact scores, and an 11 percent reduction in fatigue severity scores. And these improvements were even greater at the three-month follow-up assessment: a 47 percent decline in anxiety scores, a 32 percent decrease in depression scores, a 19 percent reduction in illness impact scores, and a 21 percent decrease in fatigue scores. The participants rated the EMT as most helpful in reducing stress, improving coping, and lessening pain, in that order.

The biofeedback findings confirmed that EMT was in fact associated with increased physical relaxation. Relaxation is indicated by an increase in baseline hand temperature as measured by the biofeedback device. During the two sessions of EMT, the average hand temperature increased by 4.9 degrees. This is a substantial increase in hand warming that confirmed the participants' ratings of reduced stress and increased relaxation during the EMT procedure.

Because this study did not include a formal control group (a group that receives either no treatment or some other form of treatment), I cannot say with complete confidence that these favorable outcomes were due to the effects of EMT. Perhaps the participants were simply going through an improvement cycle in their illness, and the gains would have occurred even without treatment. Or the understanding and attention provided to the participants during the treatment sessions may have been an important factor in their improvement. After all, people with fibromyalgia are often dismissed by their doctors as malingerers. Talking with a health professional who is sensitive to their concerns may in itself be stress relieving.

Although I did not have a formal control condition that matched the number of sessions in the EMT with another treatment or an attention control group, I did have what I might call an *informal* control group. This control condition consisted of an eight-session stress management group that I conducted on four people with fibromyalgia. The same pen-and-paper tests were used to assess improvements. I compared the results of the two-session EMT treatment with the eight-session group treatment.

In comparison to the EMT treatment, the fibromyalgia group participants received considerably more positive attention from me and others in the group. The group also received a number of proven treatments for fibromyalgia including relaxation training, cognitive coping skills, sleep improvement strategies, activity pacing, and patient education about the illness. Thus, the group comparison controlled both for the effects of simple attention and the effects of another behavioral treatment on the outcome of the EMT study.

How did the eight-session group therapy outcome compare to the two-session EMT? First of all, the baseline test scores for both EMT and group therapy participants were similar: Everyone showed high levels of anxiety, depression, fatigue, and illness impairment. After eight sessions of the stress management group, the tests showed no reduction in anxiety or depression scores, a 13 percent reduction in illness impact scores, and a 27 percent reduction in fatigue severity scores. By comparison, the EMT participants showed substantial improvements one week after the initial session: about a 30 percent reduction in anxiety and depression scores, and an 11 percent reduction in fatigue scores. Both the therapy group and the EMT group showed a 13 percent reduction in illness impact scores. And the EMT improvements at the follow-up evaluation were even greater. To be fair, a three-month follow-up of the stress management group would provide the best comparison to the EMT follow-up findings.

To sum up these comparisons, two sessions of EMT may be more effective in reducing anxiety and depression than eight sessions of a stress management group. Two sessions of EMT also seem to be as effective as eight sessions of stress management in reducing the impact of fibromyalgia. The stress management group seems to be more effective in reducing fatigue. Because this study is based on a small number of subjects, I do not know if these results will be the same for studies with a large number of participants. It's important to replicate these findings in larger well-controlled studies.

This successful preliminary study of EMT in a population that is notoriously difficult to treat both medically and psychologically suggests the usefulness of EMT for a wide range of life stresses that we all encounter from time to time. What are the psychological and emotional stressors that we face? The next chapter addresses this question.

CHAPTER 2

The American Lifestyle: Overworked and Overstressed

In the 1950s, experts predicted that economic progress, based on automation and increased productivity, would yield steady reductions in the amount of time we spend at work. By implication, leisure time would expand and improve the quality of our lives. It was estimated that by the 1990s we could choose between a twenty-two-hour work week, a six-month work year, or a standard retirement age of thirty-eight.

What a distant piece of history these projections have become! The current realities of weekly work schedules show that paid employment, rather than leisure, has become the dominant activity for many Americans. In her best-selling book, *The Overworked American*, Harvard economist Juliet B. Schor (1991) points out that, in the past two decades, the amount of time Americans spend at their jobs has risen steadily. The average working adult puts in two more weeks of work than he—or, especially, she—put in two decades ago. In 1999, the average middle-income married couple with children worked about seven weeks more than they did a decade before (Reich 2001). And current federal statistics show that Americans are working record levels of overtime as well (Walsh 2000).

Many more women are working to support themselves, now that they stay single longer. And when they do get married, women feel obliged to work so that their families can maintain an adequate standard of living. A 1997 study by Dr. Linda Luecken and her colleagues at Duke University Medical Center confirmed that women with multiple roles (worker, mother, and wife) carry the heaviest total workload, working up to twenty-one hours more per week than men. In this study, it was found that the excretion level of the stress hormone, cortisol, was significantly higher for employed mothers with children at home than it was for women without children at home. Dr. Luecken suggested that these women were unable to unwind in the evening, perhaps due to their overextended daily schedules.

Mothers who work both inside and outside the home are so common that they have their own popular magazine, *Working Mother*. In a recent issue (Cassidy 1996), the tabulated results of a survey were published, based on 563 working mothers' responses to the question "What pushes your stress button?" Nearly half said they feel stressed out once or twice a week, and 38 percent reported feeling this way more than three times a week.

In addition to actually working longer hours, the increased use of cellular phones, laptops, and beepers makes Americans feel like they are working more. So do today's longer commutes. For all the travails of blue-collar workers, the people putting in the longest hours these days are white-collar workers on salary. Their ranks have been swelled by the information economy: 60 percent of the jobs created in the last ten years are managerial and professional positions (Walsh 2000). Many of these people toil in a legal twilight zone. The law is silent on how such workers should be compensated for their long hours, if at all. Thus, the rise of work time and the loss of leisure time affects everyone: men and women, professionals and the working class.

Many people now hold more than one job just to stay financially afloat. Despite an eight-year economic recovery in the 1990s, real wages have declined. The promise of job security has evaporated for many professional, corporate, and business jobs. Even civil service positions, once considered safe and sure, no longer carry an employment guarantee. Raises, promotions, paid vacations, sick leave, and even pensions are increasingly threatened by corporate downsizing, business failures, and global economic competition. As Robert Reich (2001), the former Secretary of Labor in the Clinton administration, stated in his recent book, *The Future of Success*:

> *What do people do when their earnings are less predictable, their jobs less secure, and their incomes potentially higher or lower than before? They work harder. Not only do they put in more hours on the job; they also work more intensively.* (p. 111)

And overwork has negative health consequences. Prolonged and uncontrollable stress (either at work or at home) may result in a state called "vital exhaustion"— a lack of energy, increased irritability, and feelings of demoralization. Vital exhaustion has been shown to have health consequences, including an increased risk of heart attack. Vital exhaustion may be more prevalent in women who must cope with the demands of both work and family. One theory of stress and illness (Friedberg and Jason 2001) holds that overextended, overcommitted lifestyles may predispose some individuals to chronic fatigue syndrome and fibromyalgia. Both are common debilitating conditions that affect primarily women.

Another significant source of stress is the breakdown of the traditional two-parent family. Marital separations and divorce are now commonplace. Thirty years ago, fewer than 15 percent of all families were headed by a single person. Today that figure is more than 30 percent (Reich 2001). Single parents worry that they cannot spend enough time to properly raise their children, while working full-time jobs to sustain a modest standard of living. Half of the population now says they have too little time for their families.

In the social arena, dating has become risky with the fear of sexually transmitted diseases. Not surprisingly, nearly half of unmarried heterosexual men and women worry about contracting AIDS from sexual partners. Frustrations also arise from the difficulties of maintaining (or breaking up) intimate relationships.

The stress of such "role overload" results in emotional and physical exhaustion. Yet we rarely allow ourselves the luxury of regular relaxation intervals to recover and restore our health and well-being. Instead, we try to "fix" our overstressed lives with better organization or by working even harder.

Stress and Illness

All of these stressors can have a profound impact on physical and emotional health. It is estimated that 50 to 80 percent of all diseases are stress related. Dr. Juliet Schor's previously cited book, *The Overworked American* (1991), suggests that generalized overwork may account for the rise in stress-related disorders over the past two decades. There are well-documented connections between stress and a number of medical conditions, including anxiety and phobic disorders, chronic headache, persistent low back and arthritic pain, sleep disturbance, sexual difficulties, and chronic fatigue.

Psychological stress can trigger or worsen symptoms of anxiety, panic attacks, and disabling phobic conditions, including fears of driving and public speaking. Fifty percent of migraine sufferers cite stress as a major contributing factor to their headaches. Other chronic pain problems are stress sensitive as well. For instance, stressful life events can influence the onset and progression of rheumatoid arthritis. Psychological factors may also play a role in triggering or worsening low back pain. Restful sleep is another casualty of our overstressed lifestyles. Not only do Americans sleep sixty to ninety minutes less than is needed for a healthy, restorative sleep, they often take their stress to bed by thinking about job pressures, financial strains, and family problems. These intrusive thoughts further disturb the sleep process. The result: feelings of well-being diminish, waking concentration is impaired, and motivation suffers.

What are the long-term health consequences of our hyperactive lifestyles? Chronic and acute psychological stress have been shown to be risk factors for heart disease. Dr. Redford Williams, a medical expert on cardiovascular disease, concluded in his popular book, *Anger Kills* (Williams and Williams 1998), that persistent anger itself may be a significant risk factor for heart disease. Dr. James A.

Blumenthal, a professor of medical psychology at Duke University Medical Center, recently authored with his colleagues a literature review of psychological factors in heart disease in the pre-eminent cardiology journal, *Circulation.* (Rozanski, Blumenthal, and Kaplan 1999). The article concluded that clear evidence exists that anger, stress, depression, and social isolation contribute to the development of cardiovascular disease. Psychological stress can also promote the progression of heart disease in patients who have had heart attacks. In one study, 50 percent of patients hospitalized for heart attacks said that emotional stress was an important trigger (Krantz, Kop, Santiago, and Gottdiener 1996).

There are alarming indications that the decline in death rates from heart disease that began in the 1960s has leveled off and that rates may even be beginning to rise. For the first time in decades, the death rate from heart disease in the U.S. increased slightly from 1992 to 1993. Although we do not know precisely why these numbers are rising, increased workloads and lifestyle stress may well be contributing factors.

Recent studies on stress factors in cancer suggest that our mental state may also affect the progress of cancer. In an important and well-designed study of stress and breast cancer, Dr. M. Wirsching and his colleagues (1982) found that more than 70 percent of fifty-six patients with breast cancer tended to avoid dealing with trouble and conflict to an extensive degree. These women consistently disavowed their own interests and sacrificed themselves for others. In response to stress, these women showed more anger suppression than a control group. They also rated life events as having greater impact than did the control group. The authors of this study suggest that stress impairs the immune system and allows abnormal cells to grow unchecked. These findings have been replicated in later studies, so it appears that certain personality traits and stress responses are associated with breast cancer. Further research is needed to determine if such factors actually are a cause of this cancer.

How Stress Reduction Can Help

Stress reduction therapies help to counter the stresses of daily life, the stress of chronic medical conditions, and even the medical conditions themselves. These treatments focus on lessening the psychological and physical stress that may contribute to or worsen persistent illnesses and disorders. Stress-relieving therapies may be called by other names, including cognitive behavioral therapy, stress management, or relaxation training.

Anxiety disorders, including generalized anxiety, severe phobias, and panic disorder can all be successfully treated with stress reduction approaches. Numerous well-designed studies of cognitive behavioral therapy and applied relaxation report substantial improvements in debilitating symptoms, including persistent anxiety, panic attacks, and irritability. People with phobias can overcome their specific problems, including fears of driving and public speaking. Migraine headaches can be managed better and even reduced with relaxation techniques and biofeedback, a relaxation-oriented treatment. A controlled study of stress reduction treatment in arthritis patients showed a significant decrease in pain intensity, inflammation, and blood levels of rheumatoid factor (a marker of disease progression). Several other studies have replicated these findings in arthritis patients.

Heart Disease

Because stress may be an important causal factor in heart disease, cardiac rehabilitation programs incorporate stress reduction treatment packages. Several clinical studies suggest that the impact of stress on heart disease can be reduced with effective stress control. For example, Dr. Meyer Friedman and his colleagues (Friedman et al. 1986) at the University of California at San Francisco achieved a 50 percent reduction in second heart attacks with specific training to reduce Type A behavior, which involves high levels of anger and worry.

Cancer

Two important studies of group therapy for breast cancer patients, both of which included a stress reduction component, show a strong potential to improve quality of life. A highly publicized study conducted by Stanford psychiatrist Dr. David Spiegel and his colleagues (Spiegel, Bloom, Kraemer, and Gottheil 1989) in the mid 1980s showed that breast cancer patients who participated in stress-reducing group support programs lived longer than those who did not participate. These findings were replicated in a 1993 study headed by Dr. F. I. Fawzy of the UCLA Medical School. This study involved a six-week, six-session group therapy for sixty-eight cancer patients (with melanoma, a potentially life-threatening form of skin cancer). The therapy consisted of education, problem solving, stress reduction, relaxation, and group support. Six months after treatment had ended, the treated group showed significant improvement in immune function, when compared to the untreated control group. A six-year follow-up of these patients revealed a significantly lower recurrence of cancer and lower death rates in comparison to the control group.

Stress reduction can also be helpful for the side effects of cancer chemotherapy. Several studies have shown that relaxation and guided imagery can be used to control the anxiety, nausea, and vomiting associated with chemotherapy.

EMT Is a Proven Stress Reduction Technique

In the treatment studies described above, the typical relaxation technique recommended for stress reduction requires two twenty minute sessions a day to be effective. Even more time is needed to learn cognitive behavioral techniques, such as coping strategies, positive thinking, and imagery exercises in order to change stress-producing beliefs and attitudes. All of these methods require practice and effort over a period of several weeks or months.

In contrast, EMT can produce most of the benefits of relaxation training and cognitive behavioral techniques in only a few minutes. EMT-based relaxation can increase your feelings of well-being and reduce your stress as well as standard relaxation techniques. Also, the time-consuming process of attitude change can occur much more quickly because EMT harnesses your natural ability to lessen emotional distress and solve problems at any moment in everyday life. Why is this important? Because there is considerable evidence to suggest that minor everyday hassles (related to work, home, etc.) may predict ill health better than major life events. The ability to quickly relieve the stress of everyday hassles will not only promote better health, it will create a sense of well-being and self-control.

What are the most significant problems of daily living experienced by today's stressed American? Three general categories of problems can be described: (1) personal stressors including the emotional burdens of anxiety, depression, anger, and guilt; (2) relationship issues such as the strains of mid-life transitions, marital and relationship conflict, and job dissatisfaction; and (3) health concerns involving stress-related medical conditions such as chronic pain and headache, chronic fatigue, sleep disturbance, and sexual dysfunction.

I have seen all of these difficulties significantly eased and sometimes completely resolved with EMT. Despite the persistence of these problems, the people I advise often want quick answers. EMT will show you how to get relief *now*.

The therapeutic work that I have done on my general patient sample suggests that 75 to 80 percent of these patients respond favorably to the EMT intervention and sustain their improvements over time. EMT will rapidly reduce emotional stress and redirect thinking in a positive, rational, and optimistic way. The technique, discovered about ten years ago, can be easily learned by almost anyone. Chapter 5 will show you how to use the technique for quick stress relief and problem resolution.

How EMT Has Helped Me

EMT has helped me to better manage my own high-stress lifestyle and to solve personal problems. An example: After a long-term romantic relationship had ended, I was hurt, angry, and disappointed. The conventional wisdom is that it requires about a year to overcome the loss of a significant relationship. What EMT did for me was to make that year more tolerable, less upsetting, and more hopeful than it would have been otherwise. I practiced the technique for only a few minutes a week. EMT eased my hurt feelings about the end of the relationship and left me more optimistic. This happened every time I used it on myself. As a result, I could focus better on work and enjoy activities without the nagging intrusive thoughts of the past relationship. I have also used EMT successfully to reduce financial worries, to calm myself after an argument, and even to help me fall asleep faster.

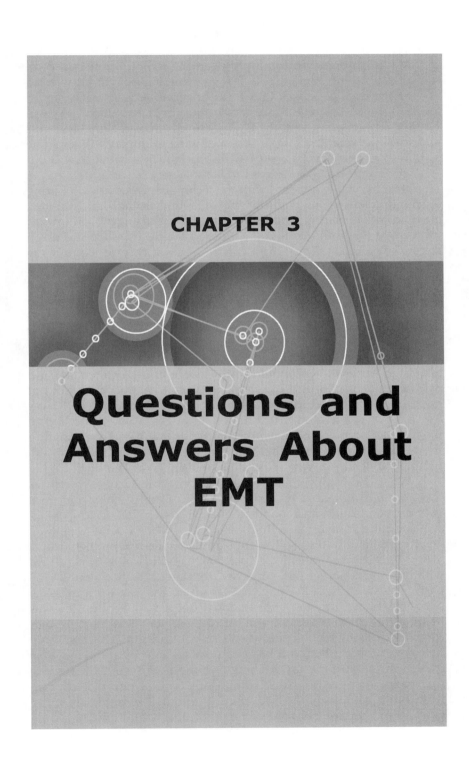

CHAPTER 3

Questions and Answers About EMT

EMT is an acronym for eye movement technique. It is a completely new method of self-change involving a rhythmic moving of the eyes or a back and forth fingertapping of the hands or knees. The process of EMT results in the rapid reduction of stress, conflict, and upsets. Using the EMT method, you can eliminate stress and solve persistent problems. The following examples will illustrate how well it can work. I'll start with a personal experience.

Several years ago, I agreed to be a subject for an EMT session. This was my first experience with the technique. I was asked to bring to mind a personal problem that I found somewhat stressful, although not overwhelmingly so. I thought of the anger I felt toward my boss at an adult sports camp where I taught massage classes on summer weekends. This was a fun and games type of job, but my boss, George, made it plain by his actions that he wanted to fire me. (This was a no pay, volunteer job!) For instance, he approved only a fraction of the weekends that I had requested for my summer schedule, while other staff typically got the schedules they requested. I was having difficulty confronting him about it because he never had time to talk and did not return my phone calls. It was frustrating!

During the EMT I focused on this personal issue and replayed one of my annoying encounters with George in my imagination and felt the emotional stress. The therapist waived his hand in front of my eyes as I followed his moving hand. Almost immediately, I felt a lessening of the tension, frustration, and anger. Toward the end of the first series of eye movements, I started to smile and even laugh. I was amazed by this result! In about ninety seconds, my feelings were completely changed from frustration and anger to laughter.

What had happened? Well, my ideas about George, the boss, had changed dramatically. I now thought of approaching him in a very direct, positive, and confident manner, rather than feeling defensive and intimidated. I imagined asking him if I had done something inappropriate or wrong, so I might learn what the real problem was.

About a week later I did just that. This time, I was very firm with him. I did not let him get away from me as he had done in the past. He reacted by admitting that I had arrived late for a massage class that I was teaching—not recently, but a year ago! So, he was holding this piece of history against me. I'm sure that he had other complaints about me, but he wasn't revealing them. This conversation broke the ice between us. The result: There was a perceptible change in his attitude toward me over the next several weeks. He was more receptive to my scheduling requests. I never discovered what other complaints he had about me, but it didn't matter. My newfound assertiveness paid off.

Did the EMT cause this change in my thoughts, feelings, and actions? I believe it did. Would the change have happened anyway? I don't think so. I had been stewing in my frustration for weeks without finding a solution. Perhaps a good therapist or a close personal friend could have given me similar advice. But I believe only the EMT could have produced such a rapid resolution to the problem (ninety seconds!) and eliminated all of the emotional stress that was attached to it. The technique removed the frustration and allowed me to find a solution—a solution that I may have known unconsciously. The EMT helped me to discover it.

When You Are Angry At the World

Chris, a petite woman of thirty-nine, was angry most of the time. Not that she didn't have understandable reasons for it. She was angry at her deceased husband for "leaving" her. She was angry at several of her late husband's greedy relatives who thought they should have been included in the will. She was angry at a friend who didn't pay back money he owed to her. Her reaction to almost any frustration was immediate anger. And she could not let go of this emotion. Why? Because it made her feel right and allowed her to avoid looking at her own stagnant life situation.

In over a year of psychotherapy, I had made almost no progress with Chris in reducing her anger. I could not penetrate that well-fortified emotional wall. So I tried EMT. The technique did work, but in a way that was quite unexpected. The new ideas that came to her were not at all suggested by me. She began to think of ways to prove "how wrong" people were to be inconsiderate, dishonest, etc. Chris imagined with satisfaction that they would get their just desserts for their bad behavior at some point. This was a vindication of sorts for Chris to imagine punishments for their behavior. Her anger diminished to almost nothing about each incident that was desensitized through the EMT technique. This happened in a fifteen-minute EMT session.

An Easy Solution for Procrastination

Nancy was a thirty-six-year-old college junior. The problem: She always waited until the last minute before studying for exams and writing up research papers. She would then feel overwhelmed by the amount of work to be crammed into a short period of time, but usually managed to complete her work on time and maintained a respectable B average.

However, she was dissatisfied with the last-minute preparations and all-night study sessions.

This type of procrastination is widespread among college students. How much conventional psychotherapy would have been required to overcome this problem? Probably five to ten sessions. Yet Nancy discovered the unconscious reasons for her procrastination and largely overcame the frustrating habit in a single EMT visit. The insights were generated by the EMT and not suggested by me, the therapist.

What was the thinking that sustained the procrastination? The thought process was as follows: Nancy's papers had to be perfect before she would hand them in. If she gave herself plenty of time to complete the paper and it did not receive a good grade, it would prove that she was stupid. But if she waited until the last minute, then a poor grade could be attributed to time pressure, rather than being stupid.

As the EMT progressed, Nancy remembered teachers encouraging her to do well and thought about a writing award that she had received only a year ago in college. Her stress levels declined as she thought of herself as more competent. If she allowed a week to complete a paper, she could do a good job without being rushed. I asked her, "But don't you need the cover story of doing the work at the last minute so you don't have to think of yourself as stupid if the paper comes back with a bad grade?" She responded with a simple but radical new idea for her: The poor grade, despite the work, would not make her a stupid person. By the end of the EMT visit, the fear of being stupid was completely removed from her thinking. And her stress about the issue had almost disappeared.

She came in the following week to say that she had completed the assigned paper and had done a better than normal job in preparing it. She did not wait until the last minute. Nancy was surprised and relieved that she hadn't forced herself through a last-minute ordeal as she had always done in the past.

Staying Calm When Your Spouse Is Unhappy

Laurie was happily married for ten years and held a satisfying job as a state auditor, which offered interesting work and camaraderie with her coworkers. But her husband had lost his engineering job a few months earlier. He had taken a new position that he did not like at half the pay. He was depressed and frustrated about this setback in his career.

Although Laurie was as supportive and encouraging as she could be, she felt guilty and extremely sad because she could not cheer him up or lighten his mood. She thought she should be able to comfort him better, but realized that her stress over this issue was hurting her and not really helping him. So she agreed to an EMT session to reduce her high level of distress. After a single series of EMT taps, she began to laugh softly and said, "This situation isn't so bad. He'll eventually rebound to a better position. I'm doing everything that I can to support him. What more can I do?" Her stress was completely gone and she felt happier than she had been in weeks.

Frequently Asked Questions About EMT

What EMT isn't

EMT is not a philosophy of living, a set of self-help principles, or a blueprint for happiness. EMT is a catalyst of change that harnesses the natural ability of your psyche to solve problems. In an EMT session, you will not see the dissection of complex personal issues as you would in a standard psychotherapy visit. The EMT method itself identifies the full scope of the problem and reveals new and better solutions.

How can EMT help me?

EMT will reduce stress quickly and resolve emotional conflicts. It can quite literally uproot negative, stressful feelings. As your distress is relieved, EMT opens up a natural progression toward resolution of your problem. Well-reasoned alternatives will spontaneously emerge. You may unconsciously "know" a better solution to a specific problem, but high levels of stress will block awareness of that alternative. Or you already may be aware of the best or right solution, but feel too conflicted or stressed to put it into practice. As the stress is removed through EMT, you will begin to recognize and accept this better solution. EMT simply brings this knowledge to conscious awareness or reinforces your ability to use a better solution that you did not know or accept before.

Rather than forcefully attempting to change beliefs and control stress, the ease and simplicity of EMT will reinforce your own natural ability to solve problems. This represents an important innovation in self-help technology. In chapter 3, I describe six different types of therapeutic change that may further explain how EMT works.

But don't such emotional changes require strong motivation, persistent effort, and self-discipline over long periods of time?

Normally, yes. However, EMT is an easy-to-use, effective alternative to time-consuming effort that will shed unwanted stress permanently, or nearly so. But you are right to be skeptical. I've used EMT on over two hundred of my clients. Seventy-five to eighty percent derived significant and lasting benefits from the procedure. Perhaps the breakthrough of the EMT technique is that it explodes the assumption that you must work hard to control stress in your life. With EMT, emotional suffering, no matter how severe, can be alleviated, often in a single five-minute session. Such rapid stress relief may indeed "cure" the problem. Short of a cure, it allows problems to be solved without the emotional pain. Is this a "quick fix"? Most definitely. Learning to minimize stress is important to functioning well and feeling happy. If stress can be quickly and almost effortlessly reduced, why not do it?

Is EMT a safe procedure?

You can safely teach yourself to use the technique for almost any problem other than trauma. People suffering from trauma symptoms should seek an experienced psychotherapist. Over nearly a decade of EMT practice, I have confirmed over and over again that emotional stress can be effectively treated within a single forty-five-minute visit and often within five to ten minutes. Occasionally, I would teach my clients how to do the technique to themselves at home, especially when the problem was stubbornly persistent. I realized that once the technique was properly taught, clients could apply it to new problems as well. The individual could continue to use EMT long after the therapy was terminated. Self-EMT yielded the same positive changes that I recorded in therapy sessions.

As for negative reactions, I have heard of only one from among the two-hundred-plus patients of mine who have used it. This individual experienced unexplained anxiety when she used the technique on several occasions. It wasn't clear why this happened, but it was easily resolved using standard relaxation methods (see chapter 13).

Thus, in the unlikely event that you experience discomfort when using EMT, it's a simple matter to stop the process and close down the session with self-relaxation.

What if you have an unresolved past trauma, but are using EMT for another problem? Is there a danger?

I have used EMT for stress problems in patients who have trauma histories, but no current trauma symptoms. On rare occasions, EMT will generate recollections of past trauma that turn out to be related to the *current* problem. *Generally these intrusions of past memories do not occur during EMT for other problems.* Usually people with past trauma are aware of what happened to them and will not be shocked by a sudden recollection. In a minority of trauma cases, where large portions of the memory are repressed and unconscious, the EMT may trigger shock and surprise. In chapter 5, I give a specific list of instructions on how to handle intrusions of traumatic memory if they should occur during an EMT treatment. *Caution:* If you are dealing with active symptoms of post-traumatic stress disorder or experience disturbing thoughts or feelings after using EMT, do not continue the procedure without consulting an experienced psychotherapist. Do not self-treat with EMT if you are experiencing symptoms such as hallucinations, wide mood swings, or suicidal or homicidal thoughts. Consult with a qualified psychotherapist.

But isn't it irresponsible to prescribe a technique that may have these dangers?

There are a variety of ways in which painful memories may be triggered. People with histories of trauma or abuse do read books on the subject, for example, *Secret Survivors* and *Toxic Parents*, and the written material may suddenly trigger memories of painful events in their own lives. TV programs on the subject of childhood abuse may produce a similar reaction. Or a self-hypnosis or relaxation technique learned from a book may lead to the discovery of past trauma. You don't have to expose yourself to presentations on the subject, but you can choose to do so and take that risk (assuming such memories exist). With EMT, you also take a small risk that you will become upset over a past event. As long as you know the risks, you can make an informed choice to use or not use the technique. (See the caution included in the response to the previous question to help you decide if EMT is appropriate for you or if more psychotherapy may be a better alternative.)

What problems can be resolved with EMT?

Almost any personal stress and its related physical and emotional symptoms, regardless of the triggering cause, can be alleviated with EMT. The technique can be applied to a variety of problems, including anxiety and worry, phobias, panic attacks, depression, persistent anger, and chronic physical tension. Medical conditions such as chronic pain and fatigue, and stress-related headaches are amenable to EMT. Important lifestyle problems also can be addressed with EMT, including job stress, midlife issues, major life changes, marital conflict, and relationship difficulties.

What are the limitations of EMT?

Although EMT is a quick stress-relief technique, it will not boost your willpower, nor will it change the basic structure of your personality. But it will reveal solutions to stubborn, persistent problems that may have plagued you far longer than necessary.

Is EMT similar to hypnosis, visualization, or relaxation training?

In my opinion, EMT is fundamentally different from other methods of altering emotional states. Although it may appear superficially similar to hypnosis—the rhythmic movements of the therapist's hands resemble some hypnotic inductions—EMT produces completely spontaneous changes in thinking and feelings that are only minimally guided by the therapist. Hypnosis is structured by the hypnotist to achieve a specific goal, but in my experience, produces very short-lived relief from personal problems. EMT, on the other hand, will resolve personal conflict and all of the stress connected to it.

Similar to hypnosis, visualization is formulated with a clear goal in mind, such as mental rehearsal to find a job or alter eating habits or improve athletic performance. But once again, the content of the visualization is largely controlled by the therapist or based on an agreement between the therapist and the patient. EMT, on the other hand, harnesses the full creative ability of the patient (with minimal guidance) to achieve personal goals.

Relaxation training and EMT do have similarities. EMT is a potent relaxation technique and can be used solely for its calming effects. In contrast to standard relaxation methods, I believe EMT produces deep feelings of calm more quickly and easily. In chapter 12, I show how EMT, as a quick calming technique, can be used instead of standard relaxation methods for general relaxation, tension release, coping with stress, and sleep difficulties.

Hypnosis, visualization, and relaxation techniques all have important applications to cope with stress and encourage positive thinking. Sometimes these methods can be useful in combination with EMT.

Why do you prefer to use fingertaps as an EMT technique, rather than eye movements?

The EM in EMT stands for eye movement. Back and forth eye movement is the original technique of EMT. And I use the eye movement technique on the rare occasions when the fingertaps don't work. I prefer the fingertap technique of EMT for many reasons: (1) It is easier to use than the eye movement method. Moving your eyes rapidly back and forth for several minutes requires much more effort than simple fingertapping. And some people just cannot do the quick side-to-side eye movements. (2) The fingertap technique is less likely to trigger adverse reactions. For instance, for people who are prone to severe headaches, the eye movements may trigger a headache. (3) I have found the fingertaps to be just as effective as the eye movements in reducing stress and solving problems.

How effective is EMT?

I have followed up about one hundred of my patients from one to twelve months after their EMT sessions. The EMT was done for a number of problems including anxiety, worry, persistent anger, chronic pain and fatigue, as well as marital conflict and job stress. About 80 percent of my patients reported that they were no longer bothered or very minimally bothered by the problems treated with EMT. Because many of these problems had been long-standing, I was quite impressed by that success rate. You would expect that a temporary problem might be solved whether you were treated for it or not, whether you received EMT or not. However, a one or two session "cure" with EMT for problems that have persisted for months or even years is more likely to be a result of the EMT itself.

Is the elimination of stress permanent with EMT?

More often than not, the answer is "yes." It is still hard for me to understand how a major emotional stress can be so easily eliminated. And I cannot say with absolute certainty that problems treated with EMT will never resurface. But in my experience, the problems either do not resurface or if they do return, the stress is much diminished.

Who can use self-EMT?

The technique is simple, straightforward, and easily learned. Almost anyone can apply it to personal issues and achieve success.

Who should not use self-EMT?

As I have stated, people with histories of unresolved trauma or current symptoms of post-traumatic stress disorder (disturbing memories of past events, nightmares and sleep problems, panicky feelings, near constant fear, and tension) should not use self-EMT. Also, individuals with dissociative disorders (multiple personality), psychoses such as schizophrenia and bipolar disorder (manic-depression), or borderline personality disorder should not use self-EMT. Why? Because individuals with these problems are at greater risk of becoming emotionally distraught. For these problems, consult an experienced psychotherapist.

About This Book

As you read the personal accounts of EMT in this book, you may be struck by the dramatic changes that take place in the person's thinking, feelings, and reactions to stress. These transformations are so rapid that they may seem incredible. Yet they did happen.

These positive changes occurred with little effort from the therapist or the client. The therapist merely set up the problem, then administered the EMT technique. The targeted problem was solved with little coaching or guidance. Follow the instructions in chapter 5 and you can do the technique on yourself. With EMT, you will discover your natural ability to purge stress and solve problems in your life. Once you have learned the technique, I think you will become convinced of how powerful it is.

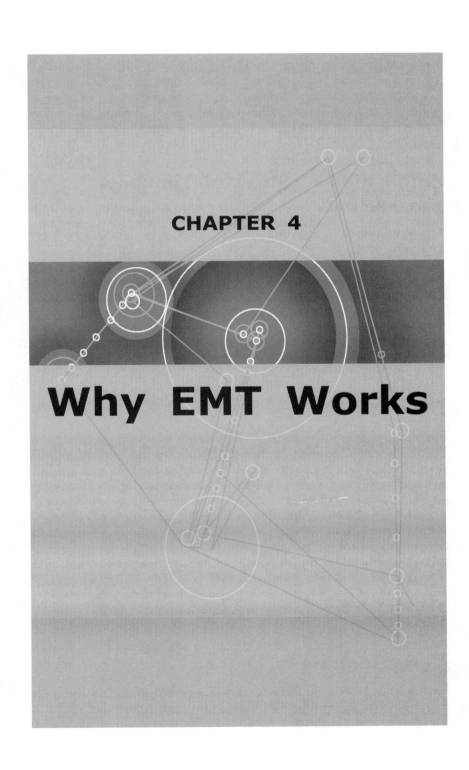

CHAPTER 4

Why EMT Works

The actual mechanisms of EMT are unknown, although research is now beginning into the psychological and physical changes that occur during the procedure. I have observed a number of emotional and cognitive changes that take place during EMT. In my experience, six overlapping factors seem to promote change.

Elimination of Stressful Thoughts and Feelings

The most common type of change in EMT, and perhaps the most intriguing one, is that the stressful thoughts and emotions simply disappear and do not return for some time, if ever. No new thinking patterns are discovered or introduced. The technique is so powerful that the individual cannot bring back the old stressful patterns, even when trying to do so. People say things such as, "I can't think about the problem right now" or "The problem just vanished." In effect, the entire range of stressful emotions linked to the problem has been removed. The problem is gone.

Deep Relaxation

Feelings of stress are eased by the profound relaxation effects of EMT. The calm and serenity may last from several days to several weeks. With follow-up use of EMT, the relaxed feeling can be renewed again and again. There is a substantial scientific literature on the benefits of relaxation, regardless of the training method used. It diffuses the accumulated tensions of the day, creates a sense of well-being, reduces anxiety and worry, helps you cope with daily stress, and improves your sleep. EMT is yet another way to produce relaxation, but it has the advantage of being quick, easy to use, and long lasting. Rapid relaxation with EMT is explained in chapter 12. It will assist you in coping with a problem even if no other positive change in your thoughts or feelings is achieved.

New Thinking

EMT allows fresh, new ideas to replace negative thoughts and feelings. The thinking behind the anger, worry, guilt, or other stress is transformed from destructive and self-defeating to hopeful and solution-focused. My clients will say, "I'm just thinking about it differently." Or they may refer to their old way of thinking as "silly." They feel removed from their negative thinking and look at it as something they used to do, but have no need to continue.

What is fascinating about this process is how abruptly the person's thinking does, indeed, change. As a psychotherapist, I never expected that feelings of stress could be so easily uprooted or redirected. For instance, people may hold on to angry thoughts because it gives them a feeling of righteousness or power. Some examples of anger-thoughts are: "If I don't get angry, I won't be sticking up for myself" or "As long as I'm treated unfairly, I'm going to be angry." If they give up these anger-thoughts, they may feel impotent or weak. Prior to my EMT training, I would attempt to convince clients that giving up anger-thoughts would not diminish their self-worth or prevent them from solving a problem. With EMT, the old thinking is often dismissed without any discussion about the reasons behind it, and new, stress-free thinking naturally takes its place. What could be simpler?

Is it ever necessary to talk about the reasons why people stay upset? It may be. In the unlikely event that the EMT does not work during the first session, a discussion of the reasons behind the negative feelings may be important. Once these reasons are identified, the individual can decide to give them up. This decision will allow the EMT to work. See chapter 5 for a full description of the techniques of EMT.

Problem Diversion

EMT may divert your attention from a problem. The distraction may last from a few hours to a few days. During that time, your ability to relax and rethink the problem improves. A good example of diversion involved one of my clients, Beth, who was hurting from chronic pain and tension. In a job-related injury, she had fallen on her shoulders and neck. Two neck surgeries only increased her pain. The pain made it difficult for her to do housework, to maintain an outside job, and to enjoy her husband and kids. It caused marital strains as well because she rarely felt well enough for sexual relations.

During the first EMT session, Beth focused on her pain while I tapped her hands (an EMT technique). After about one minute, she began laughing almost uncontrollably. After she calmed down, she explained that the taps were completely diverting her attention from the pain. The silliness of such a strange procedure amused her. The laughter relaxed her and eased the tension that had been aggravating the pain. This was an important first step to cope with the pain and restore positive feelings. And it all began with the diversion of the EMT taps.

New Solutions to Stubborn Problems

EMT harnesses creative, new solutions to persistent problems. More than a stress reduction technique, the EMT technique reveals better ways to solve practical problems. For instance, Jim, a fifty-nine-year-old TV executive, was worried about selling his house in a very difficult buyer's market. He eliminated the worry through EMT. In his words, "I no longer believed the worrisome thoughts." But he did much more than that. The EMT also uncovered concerns about overpaying contractors and landscapers for poorly done work around his home. Jim feared confronting them, thinking that they would hate him for bruising their fragile egos.

Through the EMT, he purged the fear of not being liked, and for the first time, developed an alternative plan to handle the contractors. Jim directly told his workers what he wanted done, the time frame for completion, and the amount of money to be spent. Rather than discussing the technical details of their work, which he did not understand, he set up guidelines and arranged for penalties if a specific timetable was not met. This was a realistic new way to solve a problem that had naturally emerged as his fears and worries were eliminated through EMT.

EMT-Generated Optimism

Not only does EMT eliminate stress and solve problems, it fuels optimism. After a few minutes of EMT for a specific problem, I will hear reactions such as, "It will work out" or "I can do it." Is the optimism realistic? According to the follow-ups I have done on my clients, their ability to solve problems and improve their circumstances has been confirmed again and again. The optimistic attitude endures as well. They report a newfound ability to view problems with a sense of challenge and adventure. This is yet another vital element of the success I have seen using EMT.

These six mechanisms may operate independently or in combination to produce the positive outcomes of the EMT. Clearly, clinical research is needed to validate these possible mechanisms of the EMT process. You will recognize one or more of these experiences when you learn to do the EMT to yourself.

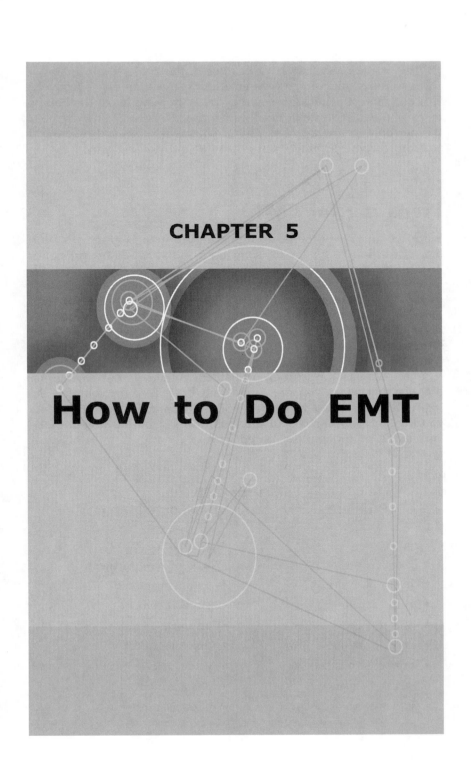

CHAPTER 5

How to Do EMT

This is the most important chapter in the book. If you follow it carefully, you can resolve emotional stress rapidly, effectively, and almost painlessly. You don't need training in psychotherapy or psychology. You don't need an advanced degree. You only need the personal desire to solve your problems quickly and a sense of adventure about solving them in a new and exciting way.

Preparing for EMT

Step 1. Sit in a comfortable, upright chair in a quiet setting with minimal distractions. Arrange for someone else to answer the phone, or turn off the ringer. Now choose a stressful issue that you would like to feel more comfortable about. This could be a job-related stress, a marital conflict, a financial problem, a family or child issue, a major life change, or any stressful emotion, such as anger, worry, fearfulness, guilt, or frustration. (*Important Note:* If you have trauma-related symptoms, please do not do EMT on your own, as instructed here. Consult a licensed psychotherapist with expertise in treating trauma.) It could be a past stressful event that still bothers you or an ongoing problem that causes you stress on a daily basis. (A more complete list of problems can be found in figure 5.1. All are amenable to EMT.) As you think about the stressful situation, focus in on the stressful feeling, image, or thought associated with it.

Figure 5.1.
Problems EMT can reduce or eliminate

- anger
- social fears
- guilt
- chronic pain
- anxiety
- chronic fatigue
- relationship stress
- stress headache
- mid-life issues

- job stress
- lack of assertiveness
- parenting stress
- discouragement
- insomnia
- marital conflict
- workaholic stress
- phobias
- physical tension

Step 2. Close your eyes and take a moment to focus on that stressful feeling, image, or thought. Can you feel the stress right now? Rate its severity on a 0 to 10 scale: 10 being the most stress, 0 being none. If you're rating is at least 4, then the EMT technique can be used. If the rating is below 4, the stress is too mild for standard EMT. However, relaxation EMT (covered in chapter 12) will help for stress levels below 4. Usually, if the problem you have selected is a significant issue in your life, you can think about it and get upset. You may want to jot down your stress rating. During and after the EMT, you will re-rate your stress level. These ratings will be our objective measure of your progress.

Step 3. As you focus on the stress, notice any related physical sensations that you feel such as headache, clenched jaw, stiff neck, stomach distress, chest pain, general physical tension, or discomforts in any part of your body. These physical symptoms can also be relieved.

The Physical Technique of EMT

Although the eye movement technique was the original method of EMT, I prefer the simpler fingertapping procedure. It is generally as effective, easier to use, and more physically comfortable. However, the eye movement technique may still be useful under certain conditions, as indicated below. Follow these instructions to eliminate stress with the EMT technique:

Step 1. Once again, focus on the stress and feel its full effect so that it matches or nearly matches the stress rating you previously made. Your eyes may be opened or closed.

Step 2. Next, rest your hands, palms down, on your thighs and tap your fingers on your thighs as follows: The right index finger taps right leg *once*, then the left index finger taps the left leg *once*. Focus on your stressful image or feeling and continue tapping in this alternating pattern. Tap at about two taps per second, *one* tap per leg. Continue the tapping for about three minutes. Don't worry about the exact timing of the taps; it's not that important.

If you prefer, ask your spouse, partner, friend, or significant other to do the taps for you. Rest your hands, palms down on your lower thighs. Ask the person to sit facing you and to tap the backs of your hands with his or her index fingers in the alternating pattern just described. If it is easier for the person to stand, ask him or her to stand behind you and tap your right and left shoulders with his or her three middle fingers in the alternating pattern described above. With my clients, I find the shoulder tapping to be easier to do and it seems to yield slightly better results.

Step 3. Once this first round of taps is completed, give yourself a moment and describe what you are feeling right now. Let's consider these three possibilities: You are feeling (a) less stress, (b) the same amount of stress, or (c) more stress. Many EMT subjects will experience an almost immediate lessening of their stress level and will resolve the problem in five to ten minutes. If your feeling of stress has decreased, go to the next heading, If Your Stress Level Has Decreased.

If your stress level has not changed or has increased, do another series of taps while focusing on the stressful image or feeling. If your stress level has not yet decreased after the second series, do one more round of taps. If, after the third series of taps, your stress level still has not lessened, turn to the heading If Your Stress Level Has *Not* Decreased, for instructions to relieve the stress. If these first three series of taps do not diminish your stress, this probably means that the full scope of the problem is unfolding, a necessary step before stress relief can begin. If your stress level has lessened, go to the next heading, If Your Stress Level Has Decreased.

If Your Stress Level Has Decreased

Identify what you are now experiencing. Your original stressful feeling, image, or thought may have disappeared. You may feel calmer. The stress-producing thoughts may look differently to you now. Or your original stress may have been replaced by another stress that is related to it. Three things have begun to happen: (a) the EMT has begun to eliminate the stress of the original problem; (b) you feel more relaxed because the technique produces relaxation apart from its ability to change stressful feelings; and (c) your thoughts about the stressful situation have begun to change to a more logical view.

The next step is to focus on the remaining stressful feelings that you have and do a second series of EMT taps. Once again, do about three minutes of tapping.

If you continue to get reduced stress after the second round of taps, do another series of taps. After the third series, rate your current level of stress about the original problem on a 0 to 10 scale. Continue with the EMT taps until the stress ratings reach a 1 or a 0. At a

1 or a 0, you should have none of the emotional stress that you experienced during the EMT. If there is any remaining emotional discomfort, focus on that discomfort and continue with the taps until all of the negative feelings are gone.

Now, do a body check: Are there any unpleasant physical sensations? If so, focus on them and do the taps until the unpleasant sensations have disappeared. When you reach these levels of improvement, your stress problem is solved—you might even say "cured." Now turn to the heading that reads EMT Success: Confirm the Change in Yourself.

If Your Stress Level Has *Not* Decreased

Either you have retained the original stressful feeling, or the feeling has changed or disappeared. The feeling may have changed to something equally stressful, or it may have been replaced by physical symptoms such as dizziness, headache, nausea, or other symptoms. The next step is to use the eye movement technique described below. Figure 5.2 summarizes this EMT procedure, which is to be used if finger taps do not decrease your stress. (*Precaution:* If you have a medical condition of the eyes that would be adversely affected by rapid left to right movements of your eyes, do not do the eye movement procedure. Also, if you are prone to severe headaches or eye pain, and the eye movement seems to trigger a similar type of headache or eye pain, stop using the eye movement. If you cannot use the eye movement for any reason, return to the taps and follow the instructions in figure 5.3.)

Step 1. While sitting comfortably, hold your head straight. To do the eye movement technique, pick two spots in the room, one to the *extreme left* of your field of vision, and the other to your *extreme right*. This could be a wall-mounted painting, a colorful book on a shelf, a TV set, a clock, etc. Now, as you think about your current stress or physical symptom, move your eyes side to side from the left target to the right target and back *as rapidly as you can.*

Do twenty-five to thirty repetitions. One repetition equals one back and forth eye movement. Then pause for a moment, and continue with another round of the eye movements while focusing on your stress. If you cannot do the eye movement, follow the instructions in figure 5.3.

(It may be easier for you to have another person, such as a spouse or a close friend, guide your eye movements. If someone is available, ask the person to sit directly in front of you and wave his or her hand from left to right and back at your eye level, about twelve inches away from your head. Your partner's index and middle fingers should be extended and your eyes should follow these extended fingers.)

If your stress level (or physical symptom) has *not* decreased after this second series of eye movements, go to step 2.

If your stress level (or physical symptom) has lessened after this second series of eye movements, do a third series of the eye movements as described above and focus on the stress you now have. Do up to seven or eight series of eye movements, but stop when your stress level reaches a 0 or 1. You are now done. Turn to the heading EMT Success: Confirm the Change in Yourself.

Step 2. If, after the second series of eye movements, your stress level still has not lessened, identify any physical sensations or symptoms, such as tension in the neck, chest pain, stomach distress, general tension, or any symptom that is associated with the stress you now feel. Focus on that physical sensation, rather than the stressful feeling, image, or thought, and *do a new series of finger taps*. If no change occurs in your stress level, repeat the tap series while focusing on the physical sensation. If there is still no stress reduction, go to step 3.

If the symptom begins to fade, continue with another series of taps until the symptom is at a very low level, or it disappears entirely. You're done when your stress level is 0 or 1. Now turn to the heading EMT Success: Confirm the Change in Yourself.

Step 3. If no change occurs in your feelings of stress after two rounds of tapping to a physical sensation, don't give up! I know you're trying to cooperate. Take a deep breathe. Relax for a moment. Now, *do up to two series of eye movements* while thinking about the same unpleasant physical sensations. If the stress levels decrease, continue with the eye movements until your stress measures 0 or 1. If your stress has not decreased, go to step 4.

Step 4. If focusing on the physical sensation did not produce a change, use the phrase *re-lax* (think to yourself *reee* as you inhale and *lax* as you exhale) as you do the finger taps until your stress drops below 4 on the 0 to 10 rating scale. You have now achieved a significant reduction in your stress. This is the best result you will get for this specific stress using EMT.

Figure 5.2.

If Stress Level Does Not Decrease with Finger Taps, Follow These Steps:

Step 1. Do up to 2 series of eye movements on the original stressful thought or image. If no reduction:

Step 2. Focus on a physical sensation associated with the stress. Do up to 2 series of finger taps. If no reduction:

Step 3. Focus on a physical sensation associated with the stress. Do up to 2 series of eye movements. If no reduction:

Step 4. Use the *relax* phrase with the taps until your stress level drops below 4. Stop the EMT.

Note: As soon as the stress level begin to decrease, return to instructions in the text to complete EMT.

Figure 5.3.

If Stress Level Does Not Decrease and You Cannot Do the Eye Movement, Follow These Steps:

Step 1. Do up to 3 series of taps on the original stressful thought or image. If no reduction:

Step 2. Focus on a physical sensation associated with the stress. Do up to 3 series of taps. If no reduction:

Step3. Think of a good coping statement for the stressful feeling. (See figure 5.4) Do up to 3 series of taps. If no reduction:

Step4. Use the *relax* phrase with the taps until your stress level drops below 4. Stop the EMT.

Note: As soon as the stress level begins to decrease, return to the instructions in the text to complete EMT.

Figure 5.4. Coping statements for EMT

I can make a plan.	I can control it.
I can do better.	I deserve better.
It will pass.	I like myself.
This is temporary.	I will get through this.
I'm okay as I am.	I did what I could.
I can accept myself.	I will do my best.
I know what to do.	I am competent.
I'm safe now.	I am well-liked.

EMT Success: Confirm the Change in Yourself

Once you are done with the EMT and your stress is minimized, you can confirm your progress. Ask yourself, "In what ways am I viewing the stressful situation differently than I did before the EMT?" The answer should be that you are looking at the situation as less threatening, devastating, or frustrating. Check the list of coping statements in figure 5.4 to see which one fits best with your new outlook. Remember that coping statement and use it if the stressful situation arises again. Next, ask yourself, "What emotions am I feeling now?" This will most likely include relaxation, acceptance, and tolerance. Negative emotions, if present, are mild and appropriate to the situation. These will include concern, disappointment, annoyance, regret, or sadness.

If the EMT has fully reprocessed your stress, then your belief in yourself has strengthened as well. You now think of yourself in a more accepting, less judgmental way, regardless of what others may believe. Your confidence in your ability to solve problems will also be improved.

Here's a good example of how effective EMT can be. This is one of many clients I've treated with EMT.

Reducing Anger Toward the Boss

Sally finished a college degree after her divorce, and now, at forty-five, had landed a position as an accountant for a local police department. However, she was extremely angry at her boss who assigned her more work than she could possibly handle. She was harassed for not doing extra work that people above her position normally did. She felt enraged, frustrated, disgusted, and annoyed about the work situation. She came into therapy seeking help to deal with the stress. Below I've excerpted the part of the session that involved EMT.

Therapist: I'd like you to get in mind the anger thoughts you just expressed: "I'd like to kill her [my boss], then the job would be okay" and "I'm stuck where I am at work." Okay. Here we go. [The therapist does a ninety-second EMT procedure.] Let your eyes open. What's happening now?

Sally: I'm feeling peaceful. I don't know how to put it in words. Like I'm drifting.

Therapist: Now, are you still thinking about work and being stuck?

Sally: Not right at this moment, no.

Therapist: When you think about being stuck at work right now, rate the stress 0 to 10, 10 being the most.

Sally: A 5.

Therapist: Why do you think it's so much less now than it was a few minutes ago? [It was rated a 9 initially.]

Sally: Because I was relaxing. Even though I thought about the problem, it was going away. I was relaxing.

Therapist: When you bring the stress back now, are you saying it's harder to get upset about it because you are relaxed?

Sally: Yes.

Therapist: Interesting. Do you still look at the job as being stuck?

Sally: Yes, because to me that's the reality of it. In other words, I'm stuck in the job situation. But the stress of the job won't affect me as much.

Therapist: Yes, you're not evaluating the job stress as badly as you did just five minutes ago. Perhaps that's what the EMT is helping you do. Let's see if we can get your stress level down further and keep it down. Now focus on being stuck at the job. [EMT procedure.] Let your eyes open, and what's happening now?

Sally: In my mind I went from saying angry words to the two bosses such as, "You are stupid," to instead saying, "Why is this happening? Can't we work it out?"

Therapist: Okay. So you took a completely different tact this time around. Rather than cursing your bosses to yourself, you thought of another way to approach them and get a better result. Let's go with that idea. [EMT.] And what's happening now?

Sally: Just talking to the manager without being annoyed or angry with her, just talking about how we can work it out.

Therapist: Taking a more humble approach. Saying, "How can I do this job better?" rather than starting with a bad attitude that she might pick up on.

Sally: Right, not an accusatory attitude, but more as a discussion.

Therapist: Let's go ahead with your new ideas. [EMT.] And what's happening now?

Sally: We continued our discussion. I just said, "I need my job but I can't continue under these circumstances. We have to change things so that I can do a better job in every area." I also said I would like to be appreciated more. She was very cooperative in her speech, but I left with the feeling that the outcome remains in doubt.

Therapist: At least you imagined a different approach to your manager. So if there is any way to help yourself, at least you turned over every stone on your behalf. Actually the scenario you just described is pretty realistic. You can assert yourself without anger, but you don't know that you will get what you want. Could you rate your stress right now thinking about being stuck at work, 0 to 10.

Sally:　　Maybe a 2. Because the way I feel right now, I could just punch out at five o'clock and leave the stress at work.

Therapist:　Which is something you've not been able to do before?

Sally:　　That's right. Does a technique like this really work? Because I'm very firm in my beliefs, and I don't think that I could follow a suggestion to believe another way.

Therapist:　Actually this technique does not involve any direct suggestions from me to you to believe in a different way. All of the beliefs that have been generated, including the ones that will help you, came from you. What I did was help you focus on the stress so that it could be reduced. Then your own solution-focused thinking surfaced as you relaxed. So you have discovered new ways of looking at the situation. I've merely facilitated that process through the EMT taps.

Sally reported in a follow-up visit that she felt relaxed the entire week after the EMT procedure. Although she did get angry at times at her supervisor, she calmed down more quickly than she had prior to the visit. Ordinarily, Sally was an extremely hyper, agitated, intense individual. To have week-long relaxed feelings, despite the constant stress, was a remarkable change for her. These calm feelings were the result of a single ten-minute EMT session. Normally, a chronically tense individual would require relaxation training, accompanied by home practice over several weeks, to achieve such a result.

The above EMT session is a good example of how quickly and dramatically the technique can work. In only a few minutes, the client's stress was reduced from a high level of 9 (out of 10) to a 2, a minimal stress rating. The client initially agreed that calm, rational thinking about her boss was desirable, but expressed *no* confidence that she could change her beliefs. Yet she succeeded in changing her negative thinking.

In a standard psychotherapy session, the therapist might have (1) explored traumatic events in the client's life that might have explained the current emotional reaction; (2) provided the client with coping beliefs to practice as a way to reduce anger; and/or (3) identified the anger creating thoughts and rationally disputed them. These methods normally require several weeks to several months of therapy to show results. In this EMT session the stressful thoughts were identified as they would be in a standard therapy visit. However, the entire process of stress relief, reevaluation of the problem situation, and generation of a new, positive outlook was accomplished in ten minutes with the EMT alone. Even the client's strong self-doubts did not impede the rapid success of the technique.

Finishing EMT When You Still Have Stress

If you wish to finish or close down the EMT session before your stress is fully resolved, use the following relaxation technique: Think to yourself, *reee* as you inhale and *lax* as you exhale, while you tap your thighs (as explained earlier in this chapter) for two to five minutes. Stop the taps when your stress level is 3 or less. This technique will relax away the stress, even if the full problem hasn't been resolved. It is better to end the EMT session on a positive note with a feeling of relief, rather than stress or tension.

Finishing EMT If You Remember Trauma

If memories of a traumatic event are evoked by the EMT, it is best to close down the session by using the *re-lax* phrase (think *ree* as you inhale and *lax* as you exhale) as you tap yourself (see the beginning of this chapter). Continue tapping until your stress decreases to a low level. At the very least, you have learned how to use relaxation as a coping skill for your stress. This is still a successful result: You have achieved a significant reduction in the stress you experience about the targeted problem. Because trauma-related upsets are often complex and unyielding, it is best to consult a qualified mental health professional who specializes in trauma treatment.

What to Do If EMT Doesn't Work

If you have made a conscientious, but unsuccessful, effort to follow all of the EMT instructions to eliminate stress, ask yourself: "Do I have mixed feelings about ridding myself of the problem?" "What will happen if I solve this problem?" "Is it all good?" "What bad things might happen?" Also, you may be directly experiencing thoughts that can block EMT, such as, "This is not going to work," "I need to feel stressed," "I don't like to feel something new and unexpected," "I feel like I'm losing control." Examine figure 5.5 to fully identify what your blocking thoughts may be. Also, turn to the chapters on worry, guilt, phobias, and anger to understand why you may be hanging on to one or more of these stressful thoughts. These explanations also challenge you to overcome your resistance to solving the problem.

Despite your best efforts, you may not be able to let go of the blocking thoughts. An example: Jeff, a forty-five-year-old widower with two kids, ages ten and thirteen, walked into my office complaining of job pressures. Since his wife's death in an auto accident two years ago, he shouldered the entire responsibility for his kids as well as working a full-time job as a real estate appraiser. The time he spent with his kids left him feeling more pressured to do his appraisal jobs with fewer work hours. He rated his job stress at a 9. During the EMT, he pictured his desk full of files. About two minutes into the procedure, he stopped my tapping and said, "Gee, you know, I couldn't concentrate on the image of my desk anymore, and I was just focusing on your tapping, but I still feel stressed and I will until I get the work done." In effect, Jeff was saying that he *had* to feel this level of pressure and stress until the work was done. If he were to relax, then maybe the work would not get done or he wouldn't feel properly motivated. So Jack's obstacle to the EMT was that he felt he *needed* to experience that high level of stress.

At this point, allowing the EMT to work becomes a choice. There is no law that says you must get rid of stress, no matter how uncomfortable and disruptive it might be. But I think it's important to recognize that there are reasons to hang on to stress and the choices you make will, to some extent, determine how the EMT works.

If you make the decision to rid yourself of the emotional stress, whatever its source, go back to the EMT and try this variation. This time, think of the stress *and* the reason that you want to hang on to it. For instance, "Anger makes me feel righteous" or "Worry helps me control the problem." Feel the full measure of stress associated with that emotion. Do a series of taps. If there is no change, add in a coping statement (select one from figure 5.4 or subsequent chapters) to help you give up the unwanted emotion. For instance, "I can function and feel better without anger," "I can solve my problem without worry," or "I deserve more for myself" (a guilt-reducing statement). If your stress lessens, then go back in this chapter to the heading If Your Stress Level Has Decreased.

Figure 5.5.
Identifying blocking beliefs worksheet

Problem I Want to Solve _____

| | **Feels Completely True** | | | | **Feels Completely Untrue** | | |

I'm embarrassed that I have this problem.
0   1   2   3   4   5   6   7

I will never get over this problem.
0   1   2   3   4   5   6   7

I'm not sure I want to get over this problem.
0   1   2   3   4   5   6   7

If I solve this problem, I will feel deprived.
0   1   2   3   4   5   6   7

I don't have the strength or the willpower to solve this problem.
0   1   2   3   4   5   6   7

If I really talk about this problem, something bad will happen.
0   1   2   3   4   5   6   7

This is a problem that can only be solved by someone else.
0   1   2   3   4   5   6   7

If I ever solve this problem, I will lose a part of who I really am.
0   1   2   3   4   5   6   7

I don't want to think about this problem anymore.
0   1   2   3   4   5   6   7

I should solve this problem, but I don't always do what I should.
0   1   2   3   4   5   6   7

I like people who have this problem better than people who don't.
0   1   2   3   4   5   6   7

Figure 5.5. cont.

	Feels Completely True					Feels Completely Untrue		

It could be dangerous for me to get over this problem.

0 1 2 3 4 5 6 7

When I try to think about this problem, I can't keep my mind on it.

0 1 2 3 4 5 6 7

I say I want to solve this problem, but I never do.

0 1 2 3 4 5 6 7

It could be bad for someone else for me to get over this problem.

0 1 2 3 4 5 6 7

If I get over this problem, I can never go back to having it again.

0 1 2 3 4 5 6 7

I don't deserve to get over this problem.

0 1 2 3 4 5 6 7

This problem is bigger than I am.

0 1 2 3 4 5 6 7

If I got over this problem, it would go against my values.

0 1 2 3 4 5 6 7

Someone in my life hates this problem.

0 1 2 3 4 5 6 7

There are some good things about having this problem.

0 1 2 3 4 5 6 7

Frankly, I don't have a problem.

0 1 2 3 4 5 6 7

I've had this problem so long, I could never completely solve it.

0 1 2 3 4 5 6 7

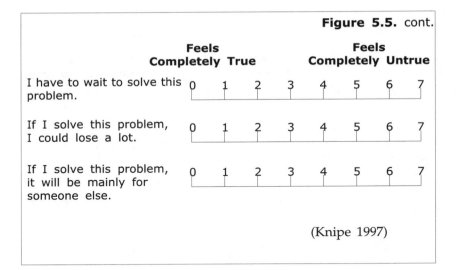

Figure **5.5.** cont.

(Knipe 1997)

Conclusion

With EMT, 75 to 80 percent of my clients have been able to achieve elimination or near elimination of their stress, combined with a new, optimistic, solution-focused view of the stressful situation. Another 10 to 15 percent have achieved significant relaxation, even if they have not changed their thinking about the stressful situation. And the remaining 5 to 10 percent have preferred the use of other, non-EMT techniques to solve their problem. Compared to conventional psychotherapeutic techniques, this is indeed a high success rate.

How enduring are the changes produced by EMT? Will the stress that has been eliminated come back? In my experience, once the original stress is alleviated, it usually does not return to its initial severity for hours, days, weeks, or even longer. But there may be a return of the stressful feelings in a much diminished form. You may wish to repeat the EMT while focusing on the recurrent stress. Don't forget to use your coping statements. At the very least, your stress about the particular problem will almost disappear for a good period of time. Even if the feelings return at a lower level, you have achieved an important degree of emotional relief that, I believe, cannot be produced by any other method.

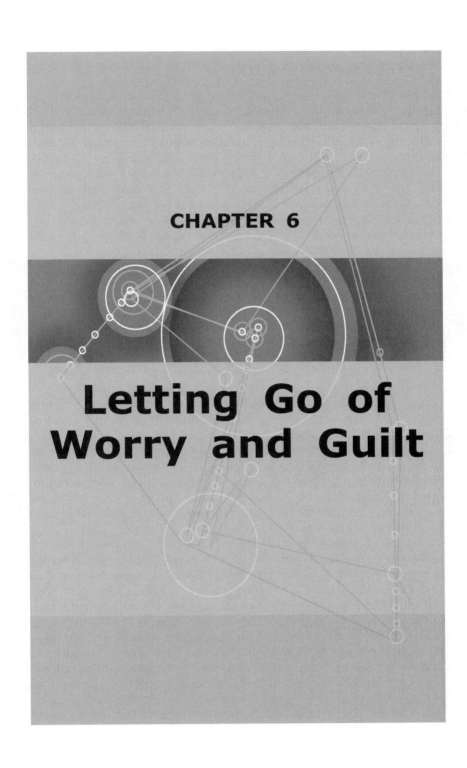

CHAPTER 6

Letting Go of
Worry and Guilt

The Nature of Worry

Persistent worry involves a devout belief in the possibility of catastrophe or disaster. Worry thoughts are prefaced by "What if . . . ," "Oh my God!" or "Just suppose . . ." Typical worry statements include, "What if my children have problems?" "Suppose we can't pay the bills?" "Oh my God, I may lose my job!" "What if he/she/they don't like me?" "Suppose I fall short (at work, at home, etc.)?" You then imagine the worst possible outcome, such as your kids flunking out of school, or the loss of all of your income, or the possibility that no one will like you. Of course these are unlikely events, but the worry keeps you focused on the worst possible case, evaluating it as horrible, awful, or catastrophic.

Dr. Albert Ellis, the founder of rational-emotive behavior therapy, believes that worry and other types of emotional stress are perpetuated by our tendency to "catastrophize" about situations or possibilities that are not as bad as they seem. Worry is sustained by two ideas: (1) the belief that if your worry becomes reality, it is "an end of the world" event; and (2) the belief that you *must* worry, unless you have a guarantee that the bad thing won't happen.

The feeling of worry, in turn, may trigger reactions such as headaches, neck aches, generalized body or muscle tension, sweaty palms, shortness of breath, palpitations, churning stomach, chest pains, restlessness or keyed up feelings, difficulty concentrating, irritability, and restless sleep.

Giving up worry may be difficult if you believe that worry will: (1) help you to solve a problem; (2) show that you care about someone or something; (3) allow you to feel that you are controlling an uncontrollable situation; (4) make you feel that you are warding off danger; or (5) give you an excuse to avoid taking reasonable risks because you might fail.

Let's challenge each of these "reasons" to worry. (1) Worry solves no problems; it only creates stress and highlights bad things that could happen. (2) Worry is not necessary to show that you care about someone. Rather than worry about someone close to you, you can be concerned and care about that person *without* the emotional burden of worry. (3) An uncontrollable situation does not change because you worry about it. With worry, you simply ruminate and dwell on the same set of thoughts over and over again. This doesn't prevent bad things from happening, but it does deter you from looking at the situation objectively. (4) Rather than protecting you from danger or threat, worry blocks constructive action designed to tackle the problem. (5) Finally, worry may become an excuse to avoid taking risks. After all, you might fail or be hurt, so it's better to worry now rather than take a risk and possibly fail later. If you let go of the worry about taking a risk, then you take the chance that you might fail, or that you *may* succeed. Remember, worry is not a reason to avoid risk, it is an excuse.

Once you identify and challenge your rationalizations to worry, then your ability to solve the problem at hand improves. If the situation cannot be changed, then you can learn to cope with it better. EMT can reduce and even eliminate your worry and direct you to possible solutions to the problem that you may not have considered.

Coping Ideas to Ease Worry

To devise good coping statements, bring your specific worry to mind and imagine what the worst possible outcome would be. Ask yourself how likely it is that this event will happen. Usually the answer is, "Very unlikely." Next, ask yourself how bad it will be if this event actually happens. If you answered "a total disaster" or its equivalent, it is time to question that evaluation. Challenge yourself by asking, "How does a bad thing happening equal a disaster? Is this bad thing totally bad in the context of my life? Is it all-important?" The idea is to downsize the negative event and evaluate it more realistically. Challenging and disputing worry-thoughts is an important element of rational-emotive behavior therapy. Here are several coping statements that will help you to believe that the worst outcome is not the catastrophe that you may think it is:

A disadvantage doesn't equal disaster.

I can make a plan.

Dwelling on the problem won't solve it.

The worry won't kill me, I've handled it before.

Worry will not change the outcome.

I will control what I can.

The risk is worth it.

Pick one or two statements from the above list and modify them to fit your particular situation. Use them in your EMT. Even if you don't believe them now, the EMT will help you to believe these new coping ideas as you incorporate them into the procedure.

Worry About a New Job

Almost everyone has experienced fear and worry about performing on a new job. Sometimes the worry can become so strong that it borders on panic. In the following EMT session, Mary was desensitized to her pervasive worry about handling a new job. In her early forties with a teenage daughter, Mary was re-entering the job market following a divorce. She had not worked in ten years. Her list of fears included the fear of screwing up, fear of getting overinvolved in the job (i.e., agreeing to extensive overtime), fear of not being comfortable at the new job, and fear of her coworkers and bosses judging her. The process of EMT resulted in a step-by-step unfolding and resolution of all of these job-seeking issues.

At the start of the session, Mary was smiling and affable despite the obvious tension in her face and the worries that she was expressing. Her goal: to have her worries just disappear. The notion of "working" on her worry so that she could cope better was not at all appealing to her. In her emphatic words, "I *should* be able to control my emotions without seeing a therapist." This visit proved to her that she was a failure at coping with life in general.

I would consider someone like Mary to be a tough customer. She was extremely uncomfortable about the session itself, had no confidence in her ability to cope with difficulties, and she was looking for a magical, no effort solution to her problem. Should I dare to believe that I could really help her? I had tried a standard relaxation technique, but as soon as she started to relax, she tensed up, opened her eyes, and said that she didn't like that feeling of "losing control" of herself. My next effort was to develop coping statements for her worry about finding a new job, but she quickly dismissed positive thinking as something completely alien to her.

Because I had just learned the EMT technique, I was reluctant to use it unless my tried-and-true methods failed. Even I was skeptical that EMT could do its apparent magic on someone with such overwhelming stress. But I was getting nowhere with my usual approach, so I decided to experiment with the new technique. I started the EMT by asking how much stress she felt about taking a new job. On a 0 to 10 scale, she rated her stress a 15! With the pervasive, unyielding stress she was reporting, I thought she might need powerful psychotropic medications to calm her. But she had already rejected medication because it represented to her even greater personal weakness.

With some hesitation, I did an initial series of EMT taps as she focused on her high intensity stress. After the first series of EMT taps, her demeanor did not change. I immediately thought, "This isn't working." Yet her reaction to the EMT indicated that something interesting had happened: she was concentrating on getting into a new job situation and dealing with new people but *without* her usual paralyzing fear. Without the distraction of this strong anxiety, she could now figure out if she felt comfortable in that setting. In her words, "I don't have to take the job, just go for the interview." This type of objective thinking, which I did not suggest, was a complete surprise to both of us. It was almost too easy. I was encouraged but still skeptical.

The EMT also revealed Mary's fear of getting overinvolved in a job by working overtime, weekends, and holidays. In the past, her tendency to overwork would trigger states of exhaustion and would cause her to take one or two days off. Would she fall into that pattern again? Could this problem be cured? I have excerpted this part of the EMT session below:

Mary: This is my problem area: Getting too involved with work [by volunteering to work overtime, weekends, and holidays]. I don't know how I can change that. It's my nature. I was just thinking about when I was younger going to school, I always wanted to be involved with every activity I could find. How would I cure that? That's a scary one, the idea of falling into it again.

Therapist: Is there some balance you can strike between getting involved versus being overinvolved? Can you think of how you might do that?

Mary: Maybe tell a boss that I've been in jobs before where more hours got added to my schedule and I ended up not having a social life or a personal life. I don't want that to happen again.

Therapist: Good, let's just start with that. You imagine talking to a boss and saying those things. Okay? Obviously it is a very sensitive issue, because even imagining it is difficult. So can you get that in your mind? A boss wants the extra hours, you're telling him what you just said. Here we go. [EMT.] What's happening now?

Mary: I imagined discussing priorities about what needs to be done first and most importantly. I understand that there are urgent situations where I might have to stay or do extra hours once in a while, but if it's an ongoing thing, then priorities have to be set up.

Therapist:	How did you feel about saying all of that?
Mary:	I felt good. I'm picturing a boss that I could talk to, that would understand. I think it's certainly a fair thing to do. I mean I'm willing to do extra time or work on some occasions.
Therapist:	I'm sure that a boss will recognize that you are willing to do quite a bit more than the average employee. You're just trying to set a limit on how much you want to do. You are tentative now, but you said something that sounded like, "Look, I don't want to go beyond a certain point." It was just a little seed of assertion suggesting that you are going to draw a line. When you think about all the stress of getting a job now, 0 to 10, where is it?
Mary:	Let's see. Maybe a 3½ or a 3. I feel much more comfortable with it.
Therapist:	Okay I would suggest that we do another session with this issue. If we get it down to a 1 or 0, then you are really going to do well.

The above EMT was successful in reducing several of Mary's fears about returning to work, although her most prominent fear, getting overinvolved, was not completely eradicated. By the end of the forty-five-minute session, Mary rated her stress about finding and keeping a new job at a comfortably low level of 3 on a 0 to 10 scale. Remember, her original rating was a 15. She returned to therapy two weeks later and reported that her fear of getting overinvolved in work was completely gone. The home use of the EMT after the session was probably responsible. A three-month follow-up, one month after she resumed working, revealed no resurgence of the fear of getting overinvolved in work.

Fear of Not Getting a Job

Two weeks later, Mary submitted an application for a job, and signed up for a work-related course. Her anticipatory fears about returning to work were completely gone. However, she now worried, about *not* getting a job. The EMT session below revealed other important job issues as well.

Therapist: Okay. You are rating the total stress about not getting a job as 5 on the 0 to 10 scale, 10 being the worst. Now when you think of the coping statement that we previously discussed, "I want to go out and do it [get a job]," how much do you believe that? Seven would be you totally believe, 1 you totally disbelieve.

Mary: I would say 6. I mean I do want to get out there.

Therapist: That's a big improvement from the 1½ you rated previously. Now, can you focus in on the job stress? Good. [EMT.] Let your eyes open, and what's happening now?

Mary: I can see myself going into a job location. I'm outgoing, I'm friendly, and I can see myself considering more than one possibility, say in a hospital situation, different types of openings. But I can still feel myself saying, "Are you really going to do it? Are you really going to walk in that door and talk to somebody?"

Therapist: All right. Let's go with that fear. [EMT.] Let your eyes open, and what's happening now?

Mary: Well, I figure that if I go for the interview, the worst they can do is not hire me. And if nothing appeals to me that's available, maybe there will be in the next week or month. After all, there are a lot of changes in job availability. If I make lots of applications to many different places, I might be asked in for an interview. Then maybe I could pick and choose if there were more than one opening, and not have to feel that I have no choice but to take a certain job

Therapist: Okay. Let's go with that thought. [EMT.] Let your eyes open, and what's happening now?

Mary: I really need to have a job because I'm not happy being out of work. I really have to go look for one. But I don't have to take a job that I don't want. If I take a job that's really bad, then I can leave it. I can see myself walking in the door of an employer and thinking, "Well, if it doesn't go well, it doesn't go well, and if it does, then it does." But if I don't get started, then I'll never know because I'll be sitting around not doing anything and then I'll be very poor.

Therapist: Could you rate the total stress about getting a job, 0 to 10?

Mary: The way I feel right now, I would say .5.

Therapist: Is that 0.5?

Mary: Yeah, right now.

Therapist: And the thought, "I want to go out and do it," 7 you totally believe it, 1 you totally disbelieve it.

Mary: A 7.

Therapist: Well, why don't we do just one more series to polish up your confidence? [EMT.] Let your eyes open, and what's happening now?

Mary: I'm thinking that I wouldn't take a high stress job. I'd make sure that I'd find something that is a regular nine to five to begin with. If I started feeling better about the job, if I started feeling better about myself, and my life was going better, I would look for more challenging work, but not now. I want to build up gradually. I'm not going to wreck my life again [by overworking].

Therapist: Yes, you're building a lot of flexibility into your job outlook now. You don't have to get locked into anything, which is a completely new concept for you. You have many options. You can transfer to another job, you can quit. Whatever it takes. But you have freed yourself from that suffocating obligation to stay at a job that is too stressful. That is a milestone for you. It's good, it's refreshing.

Clearly, this second session was quite successful in improving Mary's job outlook. Quite a change from the nail-biting dread that she had felt only a few minutes before. Significantly, she decided not to accept a high-stress job with long hours, but rather take a less hectic nine-to-five position. Once Mary bolstered her confidence, she would then look for more challenging work. She wasn't going to wreck her life again by overworking.

Examinations and Tests: Worries About Passing

Melanie had just finished a course on selling real estate and was now gearing up for the licensing exam. Despite extensive preparation, she was anticipating failing the test and worried about other people discovering the possibility of her less-than-competent performance on the test. This fear was magnified by her other concerns, including problems with her husband and children. This is an excerpt of the EMT session.

Therapist: Your worry is failing the real estate exam. You imagine people commenting, "Oh, you failed it?" As you think about it, you rate the stress level at a 9 [out of 10]. You've also told me that when you worry about the exam, the back of your neck burns.

Melanie: Right. It's uncomfortable, like the heat of a hair dryer.

Therapist: Focus on that, the back of your neck and that burning sensation. Here we go. [EMT.] Let your eyes open, and what's happening now?

Melanie: I feel it going up to my head.

Therapist: The burning is going up to your head?

Melanie: Yeah, like it's pushing up to the top of my head.

Therapist: Okay. Pleasant or unpleasant?

Melanie: Neither.

Therapist: Okay. Let's continue. Let your eyes open, and what's happening now?

Melanie: I feel the heat coming out of my ears.

Therapist: Interesting. Let's continue. [EMT.] Let your eyes open, and what's happening now?

Melanie: I'm more relaxed.

Therapist: Okay. The level of stress thinking about failing the exam, 10 being the most and 0 being none, where is it now?

Melanie: A 7.

Therapist: It's still pretty high. Let's focus back on people knowing that you failed and saying that you failed and all of that. Can you get that image back in your head? [EMT.] And what's happening now?

Melanie: On a 1 to 10?

Therapist: On a 0 to 10 scale, how much stress about failing the exam?

Melanie: A 5. I feel more relaxed.

Therapist: Now, bring the image back in your head once again, failing the exam and people commenting on it. Eyes open, and what's happening now?

Melanie: Not that I don't care, but it doesn't bother me as much right now when they comment on it to me. Because really, I'm doing it for myself, not for everybody else. I just can't let them bother me.

Therapist: Let's continue with that idea. [EMT.] Let your eyes open, and what's happening now?

Melanie: The more I think about it now, I believe the people close to me that know what's going on in my life will understand if I don't pass. And the ones that really don't know what I've been through, it doesn't really matter what they think. And they probably wouldn't understand anyway.

Therapist: Where's your stress now about failing the exam, 0 to 10?

Melanie: A 3.

Therapist: Do you feel that this is progressing to lower your stress about the exam? Or is it hard to say?

Melanie: It's hard to say. I don't know if it's the relaxation from just sitting here, or just re-analyzing the situation, or if it's the taps that are doing it.

Therapist: Why don't we go back once again to the original image of you failing and everyone commenting on it. Let's do that again. [EMT.] Open your eyes, and what's happening now?

Melanie: I tend to keep losing that thought, and now I'm starting to see the sun breaking through the window, and I was concentrating on the light.

Therapist: Relaxing?

Melanie: Yeah.

Therapist: You see, two processes are going on. First, you are relaxing. You would relax with me doing this [EMT procedure] no matter what we are focusing on—as you have observed. But the other part is that you are learning to view not doing well on the exam very differently. Now generally, if your stress is reduced to a large extent [through EMT], it's a more or less permanent change. Where would you say you are now, 0 to 10, on the worry scale about failing?

Melanie: I wasn't even really thinking about it.

Therapist: Can you bring it back.

Melanie: A 3, if I think about it.

Therapist: This is probably about as good as we are going to do today. Now you have to tell me next time whether you continue to feel this way or if the worry just comes back. Usually a 1 or a 0 rating means that the stress is gone. If you stay at a 3, it is certainly better than a 9 or a 10, but the stress may come back. So, that's clearly progress.

Melanie showed significant progress in reducing her worry about failing the real estate exam, yet she voiced skepticism about the change. Was it really the EMT that did it? In part, her skepticism is a healthy reaction to a technique that seems to work so quickly and effectively. Yet I believe it also reflects an underlying pessimism about her ability to control worry and perhaps refocus her life on a new challenge. Melanie did not return for a follow-up visit so I cannot say if her progress was maintained. But now she had the EMT skill that I had taught her to use on her own if her exam worries returned.

Worry About Professional Recognition

At forty-five, Norma was an accomplished research psychologist, yet she often doubted her abilities. She also placed demands on herself to be a "perfect" mother to her fifteen-year-old son as well as a thoroughly devoted wife. In the therapy session, her most immediate problem was a fear of interacting with her colleagues at an upcoming professional conference. Norma felt overwhelmed by her numerous responsibilities at the meeting, including speeches where she would have to respond to public questioning. She also felt self-conscious about the possibility that her colleagues would judge her poorly about the way she dressed, acted, and spoke.

Thinking about these issues, she experienced tension in the back of her neck and shoulders. Her stress was rated at an 8 level, 10 being the highest. Rather than enduring this personal turmoil, Norma wanted to believe in herself as a competent, thoughtful person who is well-liked. I have excerpted part of the EMT session with Norma below:

Therapist: Focus on the stress about the conference next week. [Three minutes of fingertapping.] And what's happening now?

Norma: I couldn't keep thinking about it. The stress gradually went away, even though I tried to keep thinking about it. Is that what usually happens?

Therapist: Yes, that is what usually happens. You can't think about the stress, even though you're trying to. Hard to believe, huh?

Norma: Yeah.

Therapist: Now, bring back the image of the stressful conference. It may not come back full force, but feel the stress as much as you can. Let your eyes close. [EMT.] And what's happening now?

Norma: Well, I went through this litany in my mind of every little thing that bothers me and then I just went on to the next thing. It's interesting. It seems like there are hundreds of little things that bother me about the conference. Walking into a crowded room bothers me. Having to speak in public bothers me. And so I am just saying those things in my mind, as I go down the list.

Therapist: Are they bothersome or stressful as you think about them?

Norma: No, I just say in my mind: This or that bothers me. For instance, thinking I have to say something intelligent bothers me. Deciding what to wear bothers me. All the things that bother me seem to flow into my mind in sequence, but without stress.

Therapist: Now, this is an important point. First you are identifying the various sources of stress at the conference. The EMT is illuminating the full range of the problem. Secondly, you can think about all of these normally bothersome thoughts without being bothered. Big advantage. Rather than dwelling on each specific problem, you can calmly think about each one and then let it go. Where would you say your stress is right now about this conference, 10 being the most and 0 being none?

Norma: A 4.

Therapist: Let's see if we can get it down to a 1 or a 0. Do you feel that you've been at a 4 or a 5, or has the stress gradually decreased over the past few minutes?

Norma: The stress seemed to come down very fast. Even the first time that you did the finger taps.

Therapist: Do you still feel the tension at the back of your neck?

Norma: A little bit, not as much.

Therapist: I'd like you to focus on that, the tension in the back of the neck and shoulders. [EMT.] And what's happening now?

Norma: I feel that the majority of the tension in my neck and back is gone.

Therapist: Continue focusing on your neck and shoulders. [EMT.] And what's happening now?

Norma: What started going through my mind is that I don't want to feel this kind of stress anymore about this meeting. It's counterproductive, it's not useful, and I would just like to get rid of it.

Therapist: Is that something that wasn't so clear to you before?

Norma: I don't think I ever expressed it.

Therapist: Where is your stress level now, 0 to 10?

Norma: I'm much better, probably a 1 right now. Who knows what I'll feel when I leave, but I feel surprisingly calm. It's interesting. Now that I've experienced not being so stressed, the idea of having it is very unpleasant. I don't like it at all.

Therapist: You become much less tolerant of feeling stressed when you know how good you can feel. Okay. Now think about this. "I am a confident, well-liked person." How much do you believe it? 7 you totally believe, 1 you totally disbelieve it.

Norma: A 6.

Therapist: I'd like you to think about the conference and think to yourself, "I am a confident, well-liked person." Connect the thought to the image of the conference. With a strong belief in these self-worth statements you will be protected against the stress returning. [EMT.] What's happening now?

Norma: Well, maybe I'm beginning to believe it more. I seemed to say those coping ideas more slowly as I went along.

Therapist: At the beginning you were just mouthing it to yourself. Now you've started to believe it. Let's do one more round, focusing on, "I am competent, I am well-liked." [EMT.] What's happening now?

Norma: If I can relax and just be accepting of myself at the meeting and other places, I can be more sensitive to other people. I think that sometimes I'm just so tense, uptight, and self-conscious about my performance that I'm less sensitive to other individuals and what their concerns and issues really are.

Therapist: And if you are not so focused on yourself and how you are perceived, you are more sensitive to what people are asking you, responding to their questions rather than just trying to look good. As you relax and focus away from yourself, your confidence will increase.

Norma: Right, you have more energy and attention to learn from other people. Your energy can be focused in different directions which is more productive. The other people at the conference have their own worries. It is important to be a good listener because people feel that they can relax and focus on their concerns, not mine. If I were relaxed, I would be a more nurturing person to the people I need to be nurturing to. Maybe not the people at this conference, but in other areas of my life.

Norma was taught EMT to reduce stress and reinforce her progress for the upcoming conference. At the meeting two weeks later, her stress level remained at a low level of 3 or 4, rather than the usual 8 to 10. She was much less self-conscious and did not dwell on her performance. Norma even enjoyed socializing with her colleagues, a rare event for her. Still, she did not feel as smart as many of the other people at the conference. However, she could now accept that possibility, rather than berate herself about it.

A Most Common Worry: What If They Don't Like Me?

Beth had always sought others' approval by playing the role of the "good little girl." Even now, in her early thirties and married for two years, she would experience wrenching feelings of guilt and worry about the possibility of not pleasing others in social situations. Her current worry focused on being asked at an upcoming picnic to participate in activities that she really didn't want to do. Not participating would trigger overwhelming guilt and the fear that the other picnickers would dislike her. To avoid such conflict, she was considering making an excuse not to go.

At the start of the EMT procedure, the stress of being asked to do things she didn't want to do was rated a 7½. During the EMT, she imagined people were pressuring her to play a game of volleyball because they needed one more person. She found herself saying no, but the volleyballers persisted. Yet Beth felt so relaxed that she could hardly hold that image. In the next EMT, she imagined saying "no" to the volleyball players and then telling herself that it's okay to say no. Her reaction afterward: "That was very effective because I said 'no' and then a voice inside me said, 'It's okay to say no.' I repeated that and it felt very, very comfortable. "I did see myself sitting alone at a table while everybody was out playing volleyball. It caused me only a little stress, but for the most part, I felt very, very relaxed. I'm comfortable with my decision now not to participate. Also, I wasn't alone anymore [in the image]. People came back to sit with me." She now felt confident that she could avoid sports and physical activities and socialize instead.

At her next visit one week later, Beth followed through on asserting her right to say no at the picnic without feeling worry or guilt. She also began to question her overall philosophy that she must always be liked and appreciated and never disappoint anyone.

Anxiety About Social Conversations

Joe, a recently married computer specialist, came into the session looking nervous and tense. After several years of programming work, he had been promoted to a systems analyst position at age twenty-eight. Despite his professional success, he generally felt uncomfortable socializing at work. In conversations, he spoke in a quiet, halting, uncertain voice, which led his colleagues to ignore him. He would then feel bad and belittle himself. Underneath it all, Joe worried about his coworkers thinking of him as a jerk, and so was very reluctant to participate in conversations. When imagining this stressful situation, he felt an uneasiness in his chest and stomach. He wished futilely that he could relax and enjoy interactions with his coworkers.

As he remembered a work situation where he spoke in that nervous, stumbling tone of voice, he rated the stress at a 7 (10 being the highest). After the first EMT, he felt more relaxed and was focusing on the fingertapping instead of the stress. In addition to relaxing him, the EMT taps were a distraction. The second EMT evoked a memory of a work situation where another co-worker tried to intimidate him by saying that his expected promotion would go to someone else. This memory caused a hot, worried feeling to sweep over him.

In the several EMTs that followed, Joe became worried and then relaxed about a number of stressful work situations. They "popped up" spontaneously during the EMT without any prompting from me. The common element of these situations was that attention was drawn to Joe, leaving him worried and sometimes angry about looking foolish. Yet, as each new situation was identified through the EMT, he was able to maintain and deepen his feelings of relaxation, which counteracted the fear he normally experienced. Finally, Joe expressed greater confidence that he could talk to coworkers, feel relaxed, and not think of himself in a negative way. The relaxation effect was so powerful that he remained relaxed without any further EMT for an entire week.

In a follow-up visit two weeks later, Joe reported that he could talk much more easily with his colleagues. He felt almost no anxiety or fear of looking foolish. He spoke in a normal voice, not the quiet, garbled tone that he feared. Rather than feeling inferior, he now viewed himself as level-headed, smart, and logical—a rarely experienced self-endorsement before the EMT.

Dissolving Worry About the Bills

Financial concerns are a major stress for many one-parent households. Debra was divorced, supported her two children, ages eight and eleven, and worked a part-time job as a real estate agent. She was plagued with worries about falling behind on the monthly bills, although they were usually paid in a timely manner. Her ultimate fear was losing her home. The intensity of the worry sometimes caused pain and churning in her stomach and may have contributed to her severe headaches.

Rating her bill-paying worries at a high stress level of 8, her first words after the initial EMT were: "What happened? I was worrying over the bills. But then I couldn't think about the worry or the bills. Now, it's just *gone*. I kept thinking to myself, 'What am I thinking about?' I was more or less just concentrating on my hands as you were tapping." This was an entirely new experience for her. She couldn't worry even when she tried. Usually she could worry all the time without trying.

After the second EMT, she believed that she *could* get through this tough time and still feel relaxed. She felt much better and stronger. With less stress, there would be less "fuel" for her severe stress-related headaches. She began to see her worrying as a manageable habit, rather than a totally uncontrollable emotion. Rather than giving her a list of coping skills for worry, which may or may not have worked, the EMT was a much more direct and powerful approach.

For Debra, the reduction in worry was quick, dramatic, and perhaps, as you read this, almost incredible. Yet it did happen. The deep relaxation that she experienced may have accounted for some of the worry reduction. Prior research has demonstrated that relaxation is an effective coping skill for worry. However, the abrupt change from intense worry to none at all in just a few minutes cannot be fully explained by relaxation. I have given numerous relaxation procedures for worry and I cannot remember a single case where relaxation alone completely eliminated strong fear or worry.

Worry About Not Getting Paid

For those who run consulting businesses, developing a personal relationship with customers is essential to obtaining a successful agreement or contract. A common frustration for the consultant arises from clients who do not pay their bills until they are pressured with threatening letters and numerous phone calls.

Howard owned an engineering consulting firm with several workers on his payroll. In business for twenty years, he still worried about underpayments on his business accounts. His stress level about the finances was overwhelming at times, triggering tension all over his body. The specific stress-producing thought was, "It will be a disaster if I'm unable to meet the payroll." Every time an account didn't pay, he worried about meeting the payroll.

After his first EMT, Howard looked surprised and said, "I was thinking about the money that didn't come in. And what would happen. I got very anxious about that. Then, for some reason, I started focusing on the tapping and I just didn't think. It just got me away from what the problem was. I felt less stress, but now that the tapping has stopped, I'm worrying again. But I can hardly believe that I was not thinking about the money for even a minute."

As he progressed to the final EMT, Howard began to think and then believe that any payment problems could be worked out. The EMT proved to Howard that he could shift his attention from this problem and even change his thinking about it. He had not been able to do this previously. When he practiced the EMT on his own, he could dampen the financial worry whenever it bothered him.

Understanding Guilt

Persistent guilt is an emotion that may keep you dwelling on the past, immobilized in the present, and unable to claim a more enjoyable, productive life for yourself. If guilt is a prominent emotion in your life, understand that this emotion plays an important role in your view of yourself as a caring, compassionate person. Perhaps you view guilt as an important motivator in helping others, including family or friends in need. Without guilt, you may reason, you could lose your sense of right and wrong or your desire to help others. If helping others is a central value in your life, reducing guilt about falling short may seem impossible. In a similar vein, you may think that you do not deserve to be happy because of questionable things that you have done in the past. Therefore, you are "sentenced" to feel guilty and suffer the loss of your current enjoyments.

If you'd like to change your point of view consider the consequences of stubborn, unyielding guilt. This emotion will not rectify any past wrongdoing, but it will keep your thinking firmly entrenched in the past. If you are a workaholic, guilt will compel you to push to your limits in career advancement, family responsibility, or helping others, so you have little or no time for personal enjoyment. This is especially true for women. The justification for your massive efforts to help others is that you don't deserve that time for yourself. Others are more important. Guilt will prevent you from claiming yourself as a priority. If you rid yourself of this excessive guilt, you will still help others (you do enjoy it), but your life will have a healthier balance between taking care of others and yourself. If your guilt is a form of punishment for past behavior, it can give you permission to do the same, wrongful actions once again. After all, you've paid for your sins with guilt. With that form of absolution you can continue with your old, destructive behaviors. Eliminating guilt for past behavior will allow you to take responsibility for past problems and deter you from repeating them.

As stubborn and persistent as guilt can be, EMT can identify and purge guilt-producing thoughts.

Lessening Guilt

"I am a bad person for what I did (or did not do)." This belief is the basis of the feeling of guilt. Demeaning yourself as immoral, indecent, or bad is a self-esteem issue. To purge these damaging beliefs, separate your behavior from yourself as a person: You may not approve of something that you did or didn't do, but you do not have to disparage yourself as a person because of it (Ellis 1973). Here are some coping beliefs for guilt that can be used to increase the success of EMT treatment:

I can accept myself, even if I don't like what I did.

I will correct what I can.

I will focus on the present.

I have the right to make time for myself.

It's healthy to let go of impossible (self) expectations.

A Problem of Guilt: Helping Others, Neglecting Yourself

Susan devoted most of her energies to pleasing her family, friends, and bosses, while devoting very little time to her own personal pursuits and pleasures. In her early forties and recently divorced, she also fretted about her (well-adjusted) eighteen-year-old daughter. Despite helping others, she still felt guilty about not doing enough. The rapid results from the EMT were especially impressive given her long history of ignoring her own needs. Yet, if you read the previous examples of EMT, then the impressive outcomes of the technique become somewhat predictable. Susan was astonished that her guilt was purged so quickly with EMT. And she could not even retrieve this usually pervasive feeling. Instead, she began concentrating on how much she loved her daughter, without any residual guilt. Although she reported pleasant thoughts about her family and friends, she doubted that these thoughts would continue for very long. Susan was convinced that the positive thoughts would disappear and be replaced by the familiar burden of guilt.

In the subsequent EMT, she focused on that pessimistic type of thinking. It gradually yielded to deep relaxation accompanied by the thought, "Even if the guilt comes back, I can make it go away. When it does come back, I'll just work with the idea that I can get rid of it for a period of time."

Despite her progress, Susan now feared becoming a guilt-free, callous, and uncaring person. She was reassured that EMT would remove only excess guilt, and leave her conscience and compassion for other people intact. The power of EMT is in its ability to alleviate stress. It does not change personality structure or moral values.

Over the next several weeks, Susan began to focus more on personal enjoyments, including reading and creative writing, without the nagging feelings of guilt. As a result, she began to experience a greater sense of balance in her life between work, helping others, *and* personal enjoyments.

CHAPTER 7

Phobia and
Panic Relief

Phobias are irrational fears of specific objects, situations, or feelings that may restrict a person's life in many significant ways.

Common phobias include fear of driving or traveling, fear of enclosed places, fear of social situations, and most commonly, fear of public speaking. (The majority of the U.S. population is afraid of public speaking.)

Phobias may be accompanied by feelings of panic. Panic attacks are sudden episodes of terror accompanied by lightheadedness or dizziness, palpitations, shortness of breath, sweaty palms, abdominal distress, and/or collapsing feelings. As the wave of terror goes through the individual, in the absence of any real threat or danger, the person wonders, "Why is this happening?" Sometimes, the panicked person will think the symptoms signal a loss of control, going crazy, a heart attack, or imminent death. Then, a fear of future panic attacks may begin. This fear of the next attack will cause the sufferer to avoid any place where he or she believes an attack will occur. These situations may include enclosed areas like shopping malls or department stores or the inside of a car. Or the fear of panic attacks may arise whenever the person is away from the place of safety, like home.

The well-documented coping statements below (Weekes 1969), coupled with EMT, will help to alleviate panic attacks and phobic feelings. The idea behind the coping statements is that panic attacks are maintained by the fear that they will occur. The fear of a panic attack triggers release of the stress hormones into the body, causing more physical symptoms and more panic. As you learn to reduce your fear of the bodily symptoms, the panic attacks will subside. These statements are designed to ease anticipatory fears and thus reduce the frequency of panic episodes. Practice saying them for five minutes a day, and use them when the fear symptoms arise.

These feelings are distressing, not dangerous.

Feelings are not facts.

The feelings will pass; they are temporary.

I will face the fear, rather than run away from it.

The fear is the result of excess adrenaline, nothing more.

I can handle any embarrassment (due to the fear of people noticing my distress).

These coping ideas can be incorporated into your EMT sessions to reinforce your progress. If your phobic fears remain stubbornly persistent, think the coping statements during the EMT series to break through the phobic stress.

Treatment of phobias and panic attacks with EMT is usually quite straightforward. It has been argued by some psychotherapists that phobias cannot be treated in isolation because other important factors maintain the phobia, such as attention and sympathy from others, avoidance of responsibilities, or unresolved childhood traumas. Although these issues may be related to phobias in some cases, I have rarely found that they are essential to the treatment and eradication of phobic problems. A more common obstacle to overcoming phobias is the individual's general lack of confidence in dealing with stress. Feelings of low confidence may convince the phobic person that he or she cannot handle the stress of a panic attack or a phobic situation. Also, the prospect of eliminating the phobia might cause the person to feel obligated to go places and do things that they now fear.

If there is a conflict between overcoming the phobic fear and surrendering to it, the EMT process will highlight the dilemma and point to a solution. Once the individual decides to take control of the phobia, then the coping statements above combined with the EMT will do the job.

Fear of Flying

Although flying is the most convenient form of long-distance travel, many people are scared or even terrified of air trips. People with flying phobias may still choose to fly and endure unsettling panic episodes during their flights. Alternatively, flying phobics may refuse to fly at all.

Patricia had scheduled a flight to Puerto Rico two weeks after her first therapy visit. During previous air travel, she experienced severe anxiety, panicky feelings, nausea, and muscle tension throughout the flight. She had never relaxed at any point during a flight even on an exhausting overnight trip. She also recalled a frightening incident when the plane dropped suddenly, causing drinks to be spilled and objects to fall to the floor. Her current stress level about the upcoming flight was rated a 7 on a 0 to 10 scale. She had reluctantly considered taking a tranquilizer in order to get through the flight, but much preferred to learn an effective non-medication technique to control her fears.

During the EMT session, she visualized her fears of flying by imagining herself in the plane before take-off hearing the sound of the revved up jet engines. Several series of EMT taps spontaneously triggered a "dress rehearsal" of the flight from take-off to landing. One strong fear that emerged involved her walking down the aisle while thinking that the plane would become "off balanced" if she lurched to the left or right. Although this fear lessened slightly while she focused on flying, it was more helpful for her to repeat the coping statement, "I can get through this," while thinking of flying to Puerto Rico. After two more series of taps, her stress diminished to a low level of 3, and she began to feel sleepy.

The quick stress reduction impressed her, although she thought the fear would spring back to its full intensity when she actually did take the flight. Two weeks later, after returning from Puerto Rico, she reported feeling much less tense on the round trip flight. And she found that the EMT was useful during the trip to moderate her anxieties.

Fear of a Heart Attack

Among post–heart attack patients, the fear of another heart attack often inhibits their usual physical activities such as regular walks, other forms of exercise and exertion, and even sexual relations. Yet, resumption of normal activities is recommended by their doctors for the two-thirds of these patients who have no heart damage (Cioffi 1991). Another common fear is that a subsequent heart attack will be fatal because medical assistance will come too late to save the patient. These lingering fears of another heart attack can escalate into an immobilizing phobia, as it did with Gwen, one of my patients.

Gwen had been traumatized six months earlier when she was rushed to the hospital with chest pain that was diagnosed as a heart attack. Since then, she had refused to travel more than a few miles from a local hospital, fearing another heart attack. Her chest pains were also triggered by stress, but she could not distinguish stress-related chest pains from heart-related chest pains. As a retired schoolteacher, Gwen was frustrated by her fear, because she wanted to enjoy traveling with her husband and adult daughter. The session below rapidly diminished her fear of traveling away from a hospital.

Therapist: Okay. You're thinking about not being near a hospital, which generates that stress and fear. Are you getting the image?

Gwen: Yes. I'm getting the feeling of fear too.

Therapist:	Good. Now I'm going to tap your hands. The stress may lessen or it may get a little more intense initially. But it will eventually fade away. Okay. Here we go. [EMT.] And what's happening now?
Gwen:	It feels good. I felt a lightening in my chest. When I get a pang of anxiety thinking, "Oh my God, I've made a mistake" or something like that, then I get a chest pain. That eased up considerably. The tapping seemed to do that.
Therapist:	All right. Let's continue with the idea of traveling on the highway away from the hospital. [EMT.] And what's happening now?
Gwen:	I felt a lightening again. In my mind I was driving along, then finally I said, "I will be all right, I will be all right," in my mind. Then I got a little more anxious, but I did loosen up. That initial fear that I was just thinking about, making that trip, it did lighten. It's amazing.
Therapist:	Okay. Let's continue. Let's see if we can fully uproot the remaining fear. Focus on it. [EMT.] And what's happening now?
Gwen:	About the same: The lightening of the fear happened when you were tapping and I imagined driving down I-284, going through Waterville, that God awful lonely spot [far from any hospital] that has frightened me.
Therapist:	Rate the stress now about the traveling, 0 being none and 10 being the most.
Gwen:	It's down around 2.
Therapist:	Let's see if we can coax it down to a 1. Intersperse the coping suggestion you gave yourself: "I'll be all right." [EMT.] And what's happening now?
Gwen:	It was good. I could feel calm and think, "I'll be all right," not every minute, but mostly I could feel the fear in my chest moving off and the lightening of the chest. I have so many chest pains that it's hard to distinguish muscle tension from heart pain.
Therapist:	But this is actually one way to distinguish it, because we're reducing the stress-related chest pains to their lowest possible level.

Gwen:	Right.
Therapist:	How much stress do you feel now, 0 to 10, 10 being the most stress?
Gwen:	This very minute? I think somewhere between 1 and 2.
Therapist:	Good. Now it's hard to say how long your stress relief will last. Perhaps a few days, a few weeks, perhaps longer. But it's interesting and surprising that you can get such a major change in only five minutes. See how you feel when you drive to Waterville and, if necessary, we can continue working on your fear next week.
Gwen:	That will be good. It will be so wonderful.

Gwen reduced her stress about traveling and the related chest pain symptoms from a high level of 8 to a peaceful 1½ during this brief visit and felt her enthusiasm about traveling return. A follow-up visit two months later revealed no resurgence of her fear of traveling. She visited her in-laws and traveled to restaurants that were not close to any hospital. One EMT session accomplished this impressive result.

Resolving a Fear of AIDS

The possibility of HIV infection and its eventual outcome, the disease of AIDS, is a realistic concern for anyone who is sexually active and not in a long-term monogamous relationship. However, anxiety about AIDS can become a disturbing phobia in which an individual dwells on bodily sensations and fears AIDS symptoms in the absence of any evidence of HIV infection. Or one may be afraid to have sex, even if it is protected.

In her mid-thirties, Deidre had been married and monogamous for ten years. She described a very intense worry about HIV infection, despite the absence of any high risk behaviors. In particular, she envisioned having HIV and feeling a sense of total failure, shame, depression, and insecurity culminating in a horrible death. She rated the stress as a 10 on a 0 to 10 scale. The HIV worry was partially due to her having (non-dangerous) chronic fatigue symptoms, diagnosed by a physician, which sometimes accompanied feelings of weakness.

During the EMT for the AIDS fear, Deidre quickly relaxed and had difficulty even focusing on the previously intense worry. She became much more certain that her persistent fatigue had nothing to do with AIDS. This resolution of her fear happened in a single session. One month later, the AIDS fear had not returned.

Resolving Fears of Bodily Sensations

This is a session for Glen, a fifty-eight-year-old married man with two adult children. For several years, he had a phobia in regard to his own bodily sensations, thinking that they signaled serious medical problems. For instance, he worried that a sharp pain in his head might mean a potential stroke, although a MRI revealed no medical condition. The EMT showed him that the symptom could be diffused and interpreted in a non-dangerous way. Within the course of a twenty-minute session, he was able to challenge his fears and learn how to relax when he had symptoms. He rated his worry about the sharp pain at a 7 or 8.

Therapist: [EMT for worry about sharp head pain.] What's happening now?

Glen: It seems to feel more like a broader headache than a sharp pain. But I still feel anxious about it.

Therapist: This is the first sign that this pain is stress-related. With only a single series of taps, the pain was diffused.

Glen: I feel like it has moved.

Therapist: If you are able to get that kind of "movability," it means that you can probably control the symptom more than you realize, just by using stress reduction techniques. Let's continue. Let your eyes close. [EMT.] Let your eyes open. What's happening now?

Glen: I felt a real sharp piercing pain during the tapping. I am feeling confused, frightened. It jolted me again.

Therapist: All right. It scared you. Let's continue. [EMT.] What's happening now?

Glen: It was interesting. I got a couple of jolts like before, but I didn't jump to the panic level that I did before. I thought the fear was a little less, I felt a little bit more in control.

Therapist: Why do you think that happened, that you didn't jump to the panic level?

Glen: I think I feel more relaxed now just trying to keep it under control. The spreading is duller, it's becoming more like an ordinary headache.

Therapist: There you go. You may not be able to control the jolt at this point, but you can learn to react less to it. Whether the jolt means something medically, or it means nothing medically, you don't have to panic or feel as much fear as you do. And when you relax, your control is much better. Fear and relaxation are incompatible. The more relaxed you feel, the less likely you are to jump to a panic level. Why don't we continue? [EMT.] What's happening now?

Glen: For some reason, it was a struggle for me to think of the pain. I was just saying "relax" to myself.

Therapist: The taps will produce relaxation. The relaxation soon interrupts your focusing on stress, because you feel so calm.

Glen: I just got one or two jolts again on the side of my head and it's funny. I don't know if it's the pain that is so bad or the fact that I react to the pain that makes it impossible to cope with it.

Therapist: That's a crucial point. The fear feeds the specific symptom. Now, the symptom may have to do with fatigue, or headache or something else. But once you are as afraid of it as you are, then you tend to get more symptoms. Greater fear triggers a release of stress hormone which in turn magnifies the specific symptom. No matter where that pain is coming from, you don't have to react as much as you do. If you stay relaxed every day for the next couple of weeks and the jolts just fade away, then they may well be stress-related. Once you get rid of the stress and the fear about the pain, the symptom tends to recede.

Glen: I believe what you are saying, it makes sense. It's just so difficult for me.

Glen's visit showed him that the sharp pain in his head could be transformed into a dull, generalized headache. This demonstrated to him that stress was a factor in his experience of the sharp pain. As a result, he felt reassured that the sharp pain did not signal an impending stroke or a brain tumor. As he continued to relax through the EMT relaxation phase, he began to think about the sharp pain as uncomfortable, but not serious. He used the EMT at home when he experienced the phobic fears.

Relieving Fears of a Horrible Death

Virginia arrived at the session looking tense and distraught. She explained that her forty-two-year-old sister was terminally ill with lung cancer and had less than a year to live. Although Virginia had never been close to her sister, she was understandably distressed to lose her at such a young age. She now sought counseling for an overwhelming fear that she, too, would die of lung cancer in the next few years. This fear was not alleviated by the fact that she had been leading a healthy lifestyle in recent years. She had stopped smoking thirteen years ago, maintained a healthy diet, and had begun an exercise program. Despite a history of alcohol problems, she had been abstinent for the last five years. Now in her second marriage, she experienced a comfortable compatibility with her husband that she had never had in her first, turbulent marriage.

Her doctor's periodic reassurance of her good health, based on complete medical examinations that revealed no cancer or other disease, reduced her cancer fear for only a few weeks at a time. Then her anxieties would resurface at a very strong and intrusive level. In the first session, I taught her a standard relaxation technique, which worked quite well during the visit.

However, she arrived at the second session two weeks later with the news that her sister had died two days previously. Although she handled herself very well at the wake and the funeral, crying only briefly, the full impact of the death was now reaching her. As Virginia had feared, her sister had died gasping for breath in her mother's arms. She was haunted by this image, thinking that the same thing could happen to her. Her fear of a horrible death was now stronger than ever.

Virginia had practiced the standard relaxation technique, and found that it helped to keep her relaxed for two to three hours a day and also improved her sleep. Rather than focusing on body pains that might suggest cancer when she was lying in bed, she focused on the breathing technique and was distracted enough to fall asleep. Despite the success of the relaxation, she was now even more convinced that she would die soon and thought that there was no reason to plan a career or to finish graduate school because she wouldn't live long enough to accomplish these goals.

Her worry dampened all of her positive feelings, including her sexual desire, and her feelings of attractiveness and love for her husband. Although she knew this thinking was highly irrational, she could not combat it in any effective way.

Often when the client is stubbornly entrenched in emotional turmoil, as Virginia seemed to be, EMT may help to break the cycle of stress and fear. She agreed to allow me to do the technique. As she imagined dying a horrible death, rating her stress at a 9 out of 10, I did a series of EMT taps. After this first series she looked a bit bewildered, but reported feeling much better. She said the horrible image of death was "sliced up" and disconnected. She could not visualize it in one coherent, frightening image. This fragmentation of the image was stress-reducing to her.

A second series of taps was done as she focused on the less threatening image, which generated some very significant insights into the origins of her death fear. First, she realized that this type of doomsday thinking was based on numerous common experiences with her sister. Her life had paralleled her sister's when they were children. They were born only eighteen months apart and people used to say that they looked like twins—dressing alike, playing with the same toys, and even beginning menstruation at the same time. "It was like we were on the same track," Virginia remarked. Also, they started smoking pot and cigarettes at the same time, although Virginia had quit smoking thirteen years ago and her sister had continued. So Virginia thought that, because her life so closely paralleled her sister's, their destinies were linked.

Importantly, Virginia used these insights generated during the EMT to reshape her thinking:

> *I thought, "I don't have to have the same life. Even if I get cancer, it doesn't have to go the same way. There are differences. I did quit smoking, got physical examinations, and have tried to lead a healthy lifestyle. My sister didn't do any of these things. Perhaps my family history is a gift to me so that I will be more vigilant about my health. I have my own set of chromosomes and genes. It doesn't have to go down the same way."*

For the third series of taps, I had Virginia think the coping statement, "My destiny and hers are not irrevocably linked." Afterward, she said that the coping statement became stronger and stronger during the taps while her stress was reduced to a 1½, down from a very strong and disturbing 9. One week later, Virginia came into the session smiling, saying that she felt much better. Her fears of cancer had subsided. Although her anxieties rose a bit on the day of her physical exam, she calmed down quickly afterward. Perhaps most importantly, her dark anticipations about dying a premature death had eased considerably. She stated affirmatively,

> *I can just wallow in this [fear of death] or I can do some positive things, like watching my diet, daily walking, avoiding carcinogens. The rest is a crapshoot. If I do get cancer at least I'll go down fighting.*

Even her voice was more resonant and calm during the session.

At her two-week follow-up visit, Virginia remained calm in session, although she had been questioned in detail the previous week by her mother-in-law about cancer in her family. These questions made her somewhat nervous, because her mother-in-law implied that Virginia was at risk. After the conversation, Virginia reminded herself that she is doing constructive things to improve her health, and with that in mind, she can ignore the potentially worrisome comments of her mother-in-law.

Rather than dwell on potential health problems, she now told herself on a regular basis, "What did I do today to prevent [potential cancer] and protect my health?" Her new relaxed demeanor allowed her to reevaluate other self-defeating behaviors as well. She felt less obliged to speak to her mother-in-law. "I don't have to be in her good graces. I don't have to please her or everyone else as I always have done."

Despite all of these improvements, Virginia said she felt "strange," as if her new behaviors and feelings were not hers. Because the psychological changes were so quick and enduring, it took her several weeks to feel comfortable about thinking rationally and feeling calm. This is a common outcome in EMT when changes occur in only a few sessions or less. I believe that the EMT initiated the major changes which allowed the other aspects of the therapy to work.

Overcoming Fears of Public Speaking

Many highly accomplished and well-regarded professionals suffer acute distress about public speaking. These symptoms may include pervasive anxiety, headaches, nausea, vomiting, palpitations, and generalized tension. Although Marissa, a prominent neurologist, gave numerous professional and public talks, she experienced high levels of anxiety weeks before a major speech. During presentations, she would speak in a nervous, halting manner, while wondering how well she was doing. She was frustrated and angry with herself about her lack of confidence. She knew it had a negative impact on her career. "You would think I would have conquered these problems by now," she said in an exasperated voice. Marissa was tired of the problem and wanted to conquer it.

Before starting the EMT, just thinking about a speech triggered muscle constriction in her upper back and her legs, which were tensely wrapped up around each other. Marissa wanted to view herself as an educator imparting information, rather than a self-conscious, fearful presenter.

Therapist: I would like you to think about giving the talk in San Francisco next month and generate that high level of stress about it, perhaps an 8 as you just rated it. [EMT.] What's happening now?

Marissa: Well, I don't feel the tension in my back. I started thinking about walking up to the podium. That was when I was feeling the stress, but after you had been tapping for a little while, it didn't seem to generate as much stress. I felt like I could give a good talk. Actually, it's funny. As you started tapping, I saw myself walking up to the podium, but now, the picture goes blank. I can't really see it and the stress became less intense.

Therapist: As the image disappears, the stress is released. Once the stress is removed, it usually means the ideas behind it have changed as well. You then start thinking in a more confident way about your speech. The image of a good presentation rises to the surface because the confident attitude is no longer blocked by your fears. That is what appears to be happening. Do you still have some tension?

Marissa: Yeah.

Therapist: Why don't you focus on that tension. [EMT.] What's happening now?

Marissa: Well, I'm less tense than I was. The picture of me giving a speech progressed. I would be able to speak effectively and spend less time worrying.

Therapist: Are you feeling frustration now that you have to confront these obstacles?

Marissa: Well, I am frustrated and angry with myself about my lack of confidence. You would think I would have conquered these problems by now. It has really hampered me. Maybe not as much as ten years ago, but it still has a negative impact on my career. And I don't have that professional recognition for my talks. But I am really tired of it and I want to get over it.

Therapist: Focus on that: You are just tired of feeling the way you described. [EMT.] What's happening now?

Marissa: I couldn't seem to think about the stress. I started thinking about the upcoming talk and how I might focus the talk to make the points that I wanted to make more effectively. I stopped worrying about what it will feel like to be up there and thought more about what I wanted to say and how to say it.

Therapist: How do you prepare for your talks?

Marissa: Well, sometimes I write it down, if it is very formal. It depends on what the talk is about obviously, but this talk will be slightly different. It is on the same data, but it's a little different perspective than the talk I usually give. Normally, I would decide what I wanted to say and in what order. For this talk I probably would not write it down. Although when I had to give a talk to the chairman of Medicine in July, I did write that down. I didn't follow the written text, but it helped me to organize my ideas.

Therapist: You rehearsed it before hand, what you wrote down for your talk last July. I have found it most helpful to write down my entire talk in advance before I present. Then I rehearse it again and again, but I don't read from it during the actual presentation. You're not going to recall the exact wording, but you have the memory of what you read and rehearsed. The strength of that memory allows you to speak more easily and confidently.

Marissa: I don't have time to do that every time.

Therapist: Well, if you are giving a similar type of speech, you probably won't have to write it down every time. You only need to make minor changes or revisions. It can make an enormous difference. If you don't prepare a written text, it is often harder to find the exact phraseology you want to express your ideas. But if it is written down, there is a point of reference, not a verbatim memory, but a point of reference. I agree, it is very time consuming and you may not have the time, but if it is a fairly important speech where your anxiety would be very high, it may be worth it. And that written preparation will help counteract the anxiety because you'll feel better anchored to your subject matter.

Marissa: Last year I gave a really good talk. I was invited to Harvard to speak to their research group. At first, I was pretty anxious, my hand pointer was shaking. Somehow, even though Harvard has some pretty impressive people, I fell into the rhythm of the talk, and I became very comfortable. There was repartee going back and forth. I just felt that it was a really good talk. I'll be damned if I know why that talk was good and other talks were awful. But I think that it is possible for me to do this advance preparation.

Therapist: The stress you now feel about giving this San Francisco talk, 0 to 10?

Marissa: It's not so bad. It was never top strength, I'd say about a 6 or 7.

Therapist: Well, that's still substantial. We'd like to get it down to a 1 or 0. When you think of the 6 or 7 level of stress, what comes to mind about the talk?

Marissa: Part of the stress is that even though I have given a similar talk before, I still am going to have to prepare for it. To be really comfortable, I'll have to prepare more. I wish I could get past that.

Therapist: Now that is a real crucial point: I don't know if you can get past that. You know why? There are very few people who give great talks without extensive preparation. Assume you didn't have the anxiety. Do you think you have that natural ability to give great talks with minimal preparation?.

Marissa: I doubt it.

Therapist:	I know a very charismatic speaker in my field. Every time she gave a lecture, I felt envious of her presentation skills. I just assumed that her skills were natural and unrehearsed. But then I found out that she wrote down everything she said. When I heard that I felt better, because it's the same for me. When I write down my talks in advance, I come across much, much better.
Marissa:	I like the word charismatic. I would like to be able to give a more charismatic talk. In order to reduce my stress to an acceptable level, then I may have to write my talks down. And just keep a template of the talk on my computer and alter it for every different situation. Maybe it will just enable me to be more relaxed.
Therapist:	Right! First of all, reduce your stress as much as possible with the EMT and then, if you are as prepared as you can possibly be, it will be more likely that you will fall into that rhythm that you experienced at Harvard. You'll feel more spontaneous and natural. My guess is that you are probably a very interesting speaker when you can get those two things [stress and preparation] under control.
Marissa:	I think that at the Harvard talk I felt spontaneous and animated. But a few years ago, if I was giving a talk, I wasn't making statements—I was asking questions and hoping that the audience would agree with me. It was awful, awful. My negative self-image and lack of confidence—it is like you are wearing big badges on your arms, "I think I suck."

The EMT eventually reduced Marissa's high level of stress about presenting papers at a medical conference and strengthened her belief in herself as a potentially competent speaker. She also prepared better for her speech. At the San Francisco talk three weeks later, her stress level only reached a 5 or a 6, rather than the usual 8 to 10. She was better prepared, much less self-conscious, and her presentation was well-received.

Removing Fears About Surgery

The prospect of surgery often triggers strong anticipatory anxieties that may begin days or even weeks before the actual operation.

Janis, a sixty-seven-year-old retired magazine editor, was scheduled for a total hip replacement operation. She had a strong fear of being cut into bits and pieces and not waking up. I had given her EMT for worry reduction prior to her surgery. This almost totally eradicated her presurgery fears. In her last EMT image, she could see herself shaking hands with the surgeon after a successful operation. The process of EMT allowed her not only to purge her fears of surgery, but also to generate confidence in a successful outcome, which indeed occurred two weeks after the EMT.

A second example of de-stressing fears of surgery: Lynn had led an active life as a wife and mother, a nurse, and a volunteer for an environmental group. Unfortunately, her twenty-fifth wedding anniversary coincided with a medical evaluation recommending surgery for removal of an acoustic neuroma, a tumor on the ear drum. She feared the surgery itself, how long she would be asleep, how her family would get along in her absence, and how much time would be needed for recovery. Lynn also felt (1) rushed to get her house in good order before the surgery; (2) guilt about leaving the household responsibility to the family; and (3) some anger about the necessity of surgery. She rated her stress at a 10, the highest level.

During the initial EMT, she brought the fear of the surgery to mind and felt a little more relaxed. She now thought: "I just have to go in the hospital and get the surgery over with, and get well fast. Get it done and get back to normal." In subsequent EMT series, she recognized that worry was unnecessary and counterproductive. Lynn now felt more confident that the doctors would competently perform the surgery, and that all she could control was her thinking about the surgery. Further EMT generated more relaxation and optimism. "I have to do this. I can do this," she stated with much more conviction. "I am going to push the worries aside because in the long run it is going to be best for me." She did feel comfortable with the doctors. They were direct and forthcoming in providing the information she needed to know. Finally, her bottom-line fears of not waking up or suffering complications were reduced to a manageable low level. With these visceral anxieties reduced, good coping thoughts, such as "Everything will work out fine" could take hold.

CHAPTER 8

Purging Anger

A nger is a natural human emotion. We all get angry at times, and we have the right to feel and express that anger. But persistent anger can become a toxic, painful, and dominant emotion that may manifest itself as resentment, indignation, grudge-holding, rage, explosive tantrums, and at its worst, violence. It may produce physical reactions as well, including high blood pressure, skin rashes, and physical tension. The scientific research on anger shows that it may be an important risk factor for cardiovascular disease.

Why Do People Stay Angry?

Anger may provide you with a feeling of power, control, or righteousness. It's a God-like emotion flowing from the notion that we can stop unfairness, stupidity, and self-defeating behavior, and regulate the actions of other people or institutions or nature itself. To give up your anger might mean giving up feelings of power and control. Here are a few examples: "If I stop being mad at my wife, then she will think that whatever she does is okay." "If I don't stay mad at my boss (or friend), I'm compromising my principles about fair treatment." "Getting angry means I'm sticking up for myself." "Of course I'm mad at myself. It motivates me to do better." The hidden message behind anger is: As long as I'm angry (at him, her, myself, them, or it), then I don't have to take a good, hard look at changing my behavior or the unrealistic expectations I have for myself or others.

If you feel stuck with your anger, here are some good reasons to get unstuck: First, tell yourself that anger hurts you emotionally and physically, and does little to change other people's behavior (or your own). Second, anger creates distance and distrust, rather than understanding and cooperation. Third, anger prevents you from understanding and dealing with the behavior of others.

Giving up anger may cause you to feel more vulnerable to your underlying feelings of fear, guilt, hurt, and self-doubt. As you fully identify and ultimately accept these emotions, your ability to resolve your anger will improve. Surrendering anger doesn't lessen your power. It increases your power, because it strengthens your ability to solve problems with open-mindedness and flexibility, and makes it more likely you will get the results you want.

Letting Go of Anger

Anger arises from demands we make on others, on ourselves, and on our situation (Ellis 1973). We may direct our anger at our spouses, partners, friends, coworkers, bosses, children, and ourselves. We have set up certain standards for how others, ourselves, and the world should behave. When these standards aren't met, we often feel disappointment and annoyance. But if you *demand* fairness, loyalty, obedience, and smooth sailing in life, your annoyance and disappointment will escalate to anger, resentment, or even rage. The general anger statement is "He/she/they *should* or *should not* do that." An anger-related belief we often have when things don't go our way is: "I can't stand it."

Albert Ellis, the founder of rational-emotive behavior therapy, has developed an effective approach to overcome anger: Challenge, uproot, and discard the demands that create the anger in the first place. The challenges to our anger beliefs take the form of questions: "Why should anyone behave fairly, reasonably, or as I want them to?" If you answer that it is better, right, or more reasonable that they do, then ask yourself, "Why must anyone behave in those more preferable ways?" Because a behavior is preferable, that doesn't mean that people must do it or should do it. What is preferable or even advisable, is not required. As you challenge your anger beliefs, dismiss and replace them with one or more of the healthy coping statements below. These may be used in your EMT sessions.

> He has the right to act in ways that I don't like. (Even in ways that aren't fair, honest, reasonable, etc.)
>
> She is a fallible human being. (Not subhuman, a jerk, a tyrant, etc.)
>
> I wish it were fair, but it doesn't have to be.
>
> I don't like it, but I can stand it. (I've "stood" it before.)
>
> I can't control others, only myself.
>
> There is no rule that says it must be the way I would like it to be.

EMT can get rid of anger, whatever its source, whether it's directed toward others, toward the situation, or toward yourself. As your anger fades, a new, more tolerant outlook will emerge. This new outlook will recognize hassles and frustrations, but without the reaction of futile anger.

Curing Anger Toward Yourself

The amount of time Americans devote to leisure and relaxation has decreased substantially since the 1970s. Why? Because we often have to work longer hours to maintain a reasonable standard of living, especially in families affected by divorce. These concerns and responsibilities can sometimes become overwhelming. And when we are overwhelmed and cannot resolve the situation, we are likely to react angrily.

Joan was a forty-two-year-old with a fourteen-year-old daughter. She had suffered through a long and acrimonious divorce from an abusive and neglectful husband. Although she had finally achieved a sense of stability and independence in her life, her energies were often depleted by a hectic and pressured daily schedule. Because of her two jobs, home obligations, and the care of her daughter, she had little time to enjoy personal and social activities. She rated the stress of her harried lifestyle at an 8 (10 is highest). Yet it became clear during an EMT session that she was adding unnecessary anger and frustration to her already high level of stress.

In the session, Joan complained about all the things she had to do into the late evening, including attending to the bills and housecleaning, knowing that she had to get up early in the morning. In her words, "Nothing gets completed, because something else comes up that has to get done." Joan was also burdened with guilt because she didn't spend much time with her fourteen-year-old daughter. Although Joan's daughter had good grades, was socially active with friends, and appeared to be happy, Joan was angry about (1) the lack of time to do things; (2) the numerous demands and pressures of her life; and 3) the drudgery that she had to endure at age forty-two. "I shouldn't have to put up with all of this!" she insisted. She didn't have the normal suburban life that she had once envisioned.

For Joan, the initial EMT was done while she focused on her dominant thought, "I don't have enough time to do things." After this EMT, though she was still very angry, she uncovered a more complete picture of the thoughts that contributed to her stress. She began to recognize that, once she had finished her list of obligatory items, she pushed herself to do even more tasks, while attempting to ignore obvious time limitations.

Usually, EMT begins to work after the first or second series of taps or eye movements. Yet Joan's stress level remained stubbornly high until the fifth round of EMT. Then suddenly she felt calmer. In her words: "I'm thinking that I don't have to get so aggravated about not having time to finish everything. I would like to complete my little projects, but if they don't get done right away, they will still eventually get done." This was the first time she could recall thinking in this more tolerant manner. She viewed the change as almost incredible.

One month after this session, Joan was able to maintain her progress. She no longer demanded that all of her projects and tasks be quickly completed, and felt much more accepting about leaving things undone if time wasn't available. Rather than racing frenetically to finish her to-do list, she was able to pace herself, feel more relaxed, and still feel productive. And she could appreciate that her daughter was doing well without the wrenching guilt she had ordinarily experienced.

Resentment Toward Coworkers

Dan, a forty-five-year-old technical supervisor at a telecommunications company, felt resentment toward his salespeople. He became incensed when a salesperson gave an incorrect service appointment time to a customer, but blamed Dan for the mistake. This had happened more than once. Dan recently declined an invitation to a party sponsored by the salespeople because he still felt resentful about being wrongly blamed. Ironically, he *enjoyed* being resentful. He could spitefully frustrate the salespeople by pleading ignorance when they asked him for a favor. Because he couldn't make the salespeople more responsible, he could at least punish them with this passive-aggressive behavior.

Although Dan easily vented his frustrations in the session, it wasn't clear if he wanted to give up his resentment or his passive-aggressive behavior. So I simply said that I had a technique that could allow him to feel better. I assured him that he did not have to change his behavior or his thinking about the salespeople. The first round of EMT had the effect of distracting Dan from his strong feeling of resentment. Instead, as he focused on the physical sensation on his hands (the hand taps), he began to feel calmer.

During the second EMT series, he became very relaxed. He thought that focusing on the taps merely took his attention away from his resentment rather than changing his resentment-producing thoughts. He did agree, though, that feeling very relaxed was preferable to feeling the resentment. And, at that moment, he didn't care about the problem with the salespeople. Over the course of the session, Dan began to view his resentment as an unnecessary burden. This shift in his thinking was generated by the EMT. I did not suggest it. Surprisingly, he acknowledged that his tendency to react as a hothead when frustrated at work was detracting from his performance evaluations, and may have reduced his chances to get a promotion. He had not previously admitted this problem to me. Dan was now interested in learning how to do the EMT when the resentment surfaced.

Over a several week period, Dan began to use the EMT taps to relax, reduce anger, and control his emotional overreactions at work. He could now see that "enjoying" his resentment and otherwise reacting with anger was not worth the ongoing discomforts of a negative emotional state and the reduced chances of a promotion. His improved outlook reflected a genuinely new approach to coping with his work difficulties.

The Angry Spouse

Newly married young couples may be thrown into turmoil if problems develop with their in-laws. Sylvia was still furious at her husband for not confronting his mother about demeaning comments she had made to Sylvia before their wedding a year and half previously. Sylvia had yelled at his mother, thinking that she was trying to interfere with their wedding plans. Although Sylvia later apologized to her mother-in-law and made numerous attempts to reconcile by sending apology cards and inviting her to dinner, her mother-in-law stubbornly refused to see her after the incident. On Christmas Day, Sylvia's husband went alone to his mother's house for a few hours. Sylvia felt very hurt about not being invited and angry at her husband for not confronting his mother. The EMT began by focusing on this event.

Therapist: [EMT given for Sylvia's anger toward her husband.] And what is happening now?

Sylvia: I feel different. I feel great. I don't hate him anymore right now.

Therapist: That quickly?

Sylvia: Yes. But I hate his mother now.

Therapist:	We will deal with that in a moment. Why do you *not* hate your husband at this moment?
Sylvia:	Why? I don't know. I feel calmer. There is no reason to hate him.
Therapist:	But shouldn't he tell his mother off?
Sylvia:	Yes, he should.
Therapist:	Okay, but doesn't that make you angry?
Sylvia:	No.
Therapist:	But you think just as strongly that he should confront his mother?
Sylvia:	Maybe I have just given up. I feel like I should just give up and let it be, because I am not going to change him.
Therapist:	There you go. If you can accept him the way he is right now, you won't be angry. But how about your losing the holiday visit to his mother?
Sylvia:	I'm still angry about that, but there is nothing I can do about it. So I might as well let it be the way it has been.
Therapist:	Because all of your efforts to persuade your husband to confront his mother have not made much difference. Okay, how strong is your anger now toward him, 0 to 10?
Sylvia:	About a 5.
Therapist:	You still have some anger left. I want you to focus on the anger toward him and we will do another round. [EMT.] And what is happening now?
Sylvia:	I feel better. I'm not so angry with him anymore. There is nothing I can do really to change him.
Therapist:	All right. But won't you lose out on the visits with his mother?
Sylvia:	Yes. But he loves his mother. I understand that.
Therapist:	Where is your anger now 0 to 10?
Sylvia:	A 0.
Therapist:	Is that so?
Sylvia:	But his mother, I really hate.

Therapist: Would you like to get rid of that anger?

Sylvia: Yes. Change that to no, I don't. Because I hate her. She ended the good relationship we had.

Therapist: Wouldn't it be better to think something like, "Okay, she is a fallible human being who just happens to be my mother-in-law. She might do this with any daughter-in-law she would have."

Sylvia: I don't know if I can believe that. I'm so angry at her.

Therapist: What about guilt? That strong guilt you have about yelling at her before the wedding. Do you still have that?

Sylvia: Yes.

Therapist: Would you like to get rid of that guilt?

Sylvia: No.

Therapist: Why not?

Sylvia: Because I feel like I did something wrong.

Therapist: Well, you could stop berating yourself about it. You will still think you did something wrong, but you won't whip yourself anymore. Does that sound okay?

Sylvia: Yes.

Therapist: Okay, when you think about the guilt, you think about the yelling incident.

Sylvia: Yes, I shouldn't have yelled at her. It would never have gotten this far.

Therapist: And what was it you said to her?

Sylvia: I yelled at her and said, "What are you trying to do to my marriage? How can you lie like that? I never said that you were trying to destroy my marriage."

Therapist: Okay, let's focus on that. Think about that incident. [EMT.] What is happening now?

Sylvia: I don't think that my yelling made any difference because she still would have been mad. But I don't think yelling is what aggravated her. I think it had a lot more to do with the rehearsal dinner. How she reacted to that when we didn't want it on the Friday before the wedding. I think the yelling was just the last straw for her. I think she was already mad at me. And I shouldn't feel guilty for that because she lied to me and I had to stick up for myself. I just should have done it without yelling.

Therapist: Yes, the idea is not to hang the entire responsibility on yourself. There are plenty of things you know she was upset about, but she just continued to blame you. So you put it in a better perspective. Much better.

Two weeks after her initial EMT visit, Sylvia reported that her persistent feelings of hatred toward her new husband had completely disappeared. She controlled her occasional flare-ups at him by walking away from the situation and using relaxation techniques. Sylvia no longer felt any guilt about yelling at her mother-in-law before her wedding, and no longer felt animosity toward her for refusing to see her since that confrontation. The loss of the relationship with her mother-in-law was hurtful, but she still was hopeful that they could eventually reconcile.

An Adolescent Learning to Handle Rejection

Jonathan, a seventeen-year-old recent high school graduate, had friends who used him for favors, such as car rides, but never included him in their activities. Then, they would boast behind his back that they had used him. The rejection made him very angry and hurt. He rated the stress level at a maximum level, 10. Yet he felt desperate to keep the superficial friendships he had. And he didn't believe that he could think differently about the upsetting situation.

Despite his skepticism, Jonathan responded well to the first EMT, stating he felt more relaxed, as if he had been "massaged." His attitude about his fair-weather friends changed over the course of the EMT. Over two sessions, he was able to generate a more realistic, less desperate coping thought about what had happened to him: "It's not that big a deal. Like it's in the past." When asked what he would do if one of these "friends" started bragging again that he had used him, Jonathan replied, "I'll just have to ignore it."

This particular session showed that EMT could be 100 percent successful even if the person initially had no confidence that he could deal with the upsetting situation. Prior to the EMT, Jonathan rejected my coping suggestions as unworkable. By the end of the visit, he was no longer upset about his ex-friends. His upset was replaced by relaxed feelings so pleasurable, he compared it to the experience of using laughing gas—this from an individual who had suffered from anxiety and mild depression since he was twelve years old. Over the next several visits, I reinforced his newly discovered coping skills with additional EMT. His more relaxed, accepting attitude about losing his friends stayed with him, despite occasional lapses into old ways of thinking.

Coping with Insults at Age Sixteen

Greg was a quiet, sensitive teenager who earned above average grades and was dedicated to skateboarding and snowboarding. He was angry at a schoolmate, and had threatened to punch him out because his schoolmate derided his skateboarding ability (i.e., "Greg sucks"). This sport was almost like a religion to him.

Therapist: When you think about the stress of your classmate saying these things about you, how upset do you get, 0 to 10?

Greg: When I think about it, it is probably a level 10.

Therapist: What is the thought that comes to mind that makes that upset level a 10?

Greg: The fact that he thinks that he is better than me. That he keeps saying this to my friends.

Therapist: Can you think about it now and get that 10 level of stress? Good. Let your eyes close. [EMT.] Let your eyes open, and what's happening now?

Greg: I'm relaxed, but I don't know if the upset is less. I think if I left here, I could be really angry. I'm not having angry thoughts, but I know if I see him again, I will be mad at him.

Therapist: Can you imagine seeing him again right now and getting stressed about it? Let your eyes close, imagine seeing him again, getting angry all over again. Just think once again about him believing he is better than you. [EMT.] Let your eyes open, and what's happening now?

Greg: I'm more relaxed. I can't really think about it.

Therapist: Where is your stress now, 0 to 10?

Greg: A 3.

Therapist: Is this a little bit disconcerting, the idea that you can't get angry about this?

Greg: Yeah.

Therapist: You were hoping you still could get angry, huh? I took away your anger, and you want to be angry. And you want to be angry because . . .

Greg: Because this problem will keep going on. I don't know if I have to beat him up or just ignore him.

Therapist: Now, the worst thing that could happen if you're not angry is what?

Greg: I won't defend myself, and people will think I'm a wimp.

Therapist: Anyone can be thought of as a wimp. Arnold Schwarznegger could be thought of as a wimp.

Greg: You *can't* say he's a wimp.

Therapist: Okay. Arnold Schwarznegger is a wimp. I just said it.

Greg: To his face?

Therapist: No way. Behind his back, of course. Actually that's a good point about how criticism can affect people. A champion prize-fighter, about twenty years ago, was ready to kill anyone who criticized him. You know why? Because he didn't respect himself. Even though he won the heavyweight championship, he still felt that he wasn't good enough. Which is what you are doing to yourself right here. So let's look at that. The worst thing that could happen if you don't get angry is that people will call you a wimp, and you won't fight back. Are you worried now that you won't be able to get angry?

Greg: I'm just worried that I'll get humiliated if he insults me and I don't fight him.

Greg felt he *must* be angry and humiliated about a verbal put-down. Without these feelings, he thought he wouldn't defend himself. If he didn't defend himself, then he would think of himself as a wimp and so might others. His homework was to do the EMT when he was angry and upset, not to take away those emotions, but just to get relaxed so that he would tolerate the stress better. This session showed that if you *want* to stay upset, EMT will identify the reasons why. Once you look at these reasons, you can decide if they are still important to you. If you want to give up the stress, EMT will help you do that.

Identifying the Full Problem

EMT will help you to define all of the important aspects of the problem you wish to solve. Usually the full scope of the problem is anchored in recent events in your life. Occasionally, however, recall of an important childhood experience will be triggered by the EMT procedure. The experience will have an important bearing on the current problem and will figure into its successful resolution.

Bill, an engineering supervisor in his early fifties, worked at a research laboratory. Although he had enjoyed this job for the past fifteen years, he was frustrated by the poor management structure. The EMT revealed that the anger he felt toward his boss and coworkers about their substandard job performance had a childhood connection. Bill's thoughts drifted back to elementary school, third or fourth grade. He remembered a boy who used to drive him crazy—and who looked very much like one of his current coworkers. Bill was always told by his parents never to hit or bother anyone. This classmate heckled him and behaved in bizarre ways (like his coworker did now). Bill remembered that he had to put up with the kid's tormenting behavior and was miserable over it. And now he was letting that happen to himself again as an adult.

Further EMT evoked more childhood memories. Bill was taught it was wrong to express his feelings because it could upset someone or even make that person sick. He always heard from his father, "Don't get your mother sick. She's got enough problems. Don't let her worry about you now." And his mother would convey the same message, telling Bill, "Your father works so hard, he needs to be able to relax when he comes home." His father's relaxation time involved withdrawing from the family, so Bill never had much of a relationship with him.

The EMT encouraged Bill to believe that he had the right to feel the anger he had suppressed as an unacceptable emotion since childhood. Only now the anger was so strong and persistent Bill was afraid he would lose control if he expressed it. Although Bill's problem was connected to childhood memories, his current anger reflected a self-inflicted demand that he control situations that, he acknowledged, were impossible for him to control. With home practice of EMT and anger coping statements, he learned to lessen his expectations that other people, particularly his coworkers, behave competently and fairly. The EMT became an effective relaxation technique as well, although it did not completely resolve his anger problem. Fortunately, this incomplete response to the EMT is the exception rather than the rule. EMT does not alleviate every stress in every individual. Yet, even in its limited form, it helped to identify and partially resolve Bill's smoldering anger.

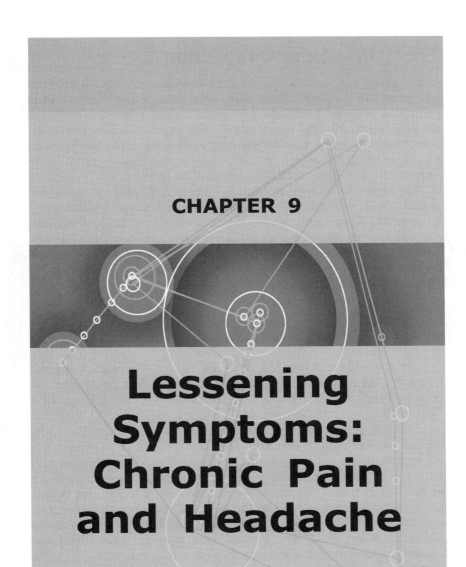

CHAPTER 9

Lessening Symptoms: Chronic Pain and Headache

The Pain-Stress Connection

Chronic pain is a fruitful area for EMT treatment. Persistent pain can take many forms: severe headaches, back pain, arthritic pain, cancer pain, pain associated with chronic fatigue, or any other pain that does not respond to medical intervention. Pain and stress are often interconnected. Persistent pain will trigger emotional stress and physical tension, and that tension, in turn, may increase pain intensity. In some cases, stress is an important cause of pain.

You may be unaware of how the stress generated by upsets and negative feelings trigger physical reactions, such as pain, tension, and fatigue. EMT can demonstrate the important connections between stress and pain symptoms, often within a few minutes. Once the connection is identified, you can then (1) alleviate the stressful emotions and physical tension; (2) generate relaxation and feelings of well-being; and ultimately, (3) ease pain symptoms.

Demonstrating the Pain-Stress Connection

In the following two cases, the individuals I treated discovered through EMT how stress and tension increased their pain and compromised their daily functioning above and beyond the impact of the pain itself.

Wendy was ordinarily optimistic and cheerful. She liked caring for her husband and two children, and at age thirty-three, had enjoyed working as a teacher for handicapped children. Then, one icy winter afternoon, she was involved in an accident. A car struck the rearend of her van. Wendy suffered whiplash injuries and had to stop working due to severe pain in her neck and shoulders. Progress in her worker's compensation case was slow. Wendy was frustrated and angry when she came to my office for treatment. I used EMT as a potential remedy for the stress and pain she suffered.

Therapist: You are angry at your attorney, angry at your employer, and angry at the "system," and you rate the total anger at 10, the highest level. Why are you angry? You were told to go back to work, but your boss won't let you work. Your rights as a job-injured worker are being ignored, and finally, you are sick of hurting. Routine things you want to do, like carrying around the baby, are difficult because the pain flares up. Okay. Let's see if we can lessen your anger. When you think about being angry at the lawyer, is there an image that comes to mind?

Wendy: I just feel like I got the wrong lawyer.

Therapist: All right, let's focus on that. I'll tap your hands. Think to yourself that you've got the wrong lawyer, and I'm going to tap your hands. [EMT.] Let your eyes open, and what's happening now?

Wendy: The pain is still bad through my neck and my shoulders, and it's shooting down my back. It just got worse.

Therapist: Just as we were doing this, it got worse?

Wendy: Yes.

Therapist: Okay. I think we're beginning to identify a pain-stress connection. You think about the lawyer, you get more pain. Let's go with the pain that you're feeling. Just focus on that. [EMT.] Eyes open, and what's happening now?

Wendy: Same thing. Just excruciating pain through my neck, shoulders, and shooting down my back.

Therapist: Okay. I'm going to tap your knees this time. Focus on your pain once again. [EMT.] And what's happening now?

Wendy: This is a surprise. I guess it makes me feel relaxed because I feel at ease now, and the pain is less.

Therapist: Good. Continue focusing on the pain. [EMT.] Let your eyes open, and what's happening now?

Wendy: Same. I feel relaxed, but the pain is still underlying. I'm more aware of the pain.

Therapist: Before you were more focused on the stress, and now you've gotten back to the pain?

Wendy: Yes.

Therapist: But you're continuing to relax?

Wendy: Yes.

Therapist: I'd like you to focus again on being angry at the lawyer. The risk is that you may get another flare-up of pain. But what I want to do is clear the anger out of your system so that there is no anger left to increase your pain. Okay. Focus on that. [EMT.] And what's happening now?

Wendy: The pain is more intense again.

Therapist: Really? So the thought of the lawyer disappeared, and you experienced the pain. Let's go back to focusing on the pain and see if we can encourage the relaxation as before. [EMT.] Let your eyes open, and what's happening now?

Wendy: I'm getting more relaxed again, but the pain is still there.

Therapist: Good. Let's continue. [EMT.] What's happening now?

Wendy: I'm getting more relaxed. The pain is more manageable, but it is still there.

From this EMT session, Wendy recognized how anger aggravated her painful condition. When the EMT procedure focused on the pain, she relaxed and felt less pain. Several months later, when the stress of the legal situation had subsided and her physical therapy for pain had progressed, the EMT produced deeper relaxation and more substantial pain relief. Ultimately, she was able to resume the work she enjoyed with handicapped children.

This next example also illustrates the importance of the pain-stress connection. Martin was a well-known chef with a national reputation. Ten years previously, he had suffered a back injury at work while lifting a two hundred pound pot. He resumed work but experienced increasingly severe back pain that eventually confined him to bed rest. Subsequently, Martin underwent back surgery and felt almost back to normal for the next several years. He participated in vigorous sports, including downhill ski racing and field hockey. Despite occasional pain flare-ups, a combination of physical therapy and medication helped him to maintain his busy work and recreation schedule. Unfortunately, he suffered a second back injury, again at work, as he was taking a heavy tray out of the oven. He became debilitated a second time, underwent a second surgery, but experienced only temporary relief. A third surgery aggravated his low back pain, which now radiated into his right leg.

When Martin came to see me he was twisted up in pain and walked haltingly with a cane. He was angry about his condition, angry at his doctors for the failed surgeries, and worried about his strained financial situation and marital problems—all related to his injury. He had lost interest in activities he used to enjoy and acknowledged he was very depressed. Having long experience with treating back pain, I knew that tension and stress were aggravating his pain. I suggested that a simple relaxation procedure might help him to feel better, but he insisted that only returning to work or improving his financial situation could ease the distress he felt. So adamant was he that I began to doubt that he would agree to a relaxation exercise.

Despite Martin's reservations, I finally persuaded him to participate in a brief EMT tap procedure that would require only a few minutes if it were to succeed. I began tapping while he focused on the tension in his back. Almost immediately, I could see his shoulders begin to loosen and relax. After about a minute and a half, he said, "Something is happening. I feel the tension draining out of me." He was noticeably surprised and agreed to let the procedure continue. After only five minutes, he felt ready to fall asleep, something that rarely happened at night when he wanted to sleep.

His newfound sense of calm allowed him to admit that he was very tense about his pain and limitations. Martin was favoring certain muscles, which in turn caused generalized tension and increased pain in other muscles. This pain-inducing process distorted his posture and led him to use the cane, reinforcing rather than correcting the misalignment of his muscles. I showed him how to do the taps for home use to release muscle tension and emotional stress.

Martin did not return for a second visit, so I do not know if he followed up on the EMT. My sense was that his all-or-nothing thinking about being either totally functional or horribly impaired was unlikely to change for more than a brief interval to a more realistic, flexible belief about coping with his ongoing limitations. Martin's narrow view of what was acceptable for well-being and happiness was likely to sustain his depressed, pessimistic outlook. Yet I believe I offered him a choice through the EMT training. A choice to be less tense, less depressed, and ultimately more hopeful about life with limitations that are unfortunate, but not necessarily devastating.

Eliminating Tension Can Reduce Pain

Physical tension may be naturally high in some people, regardless of the stress, or lack of it, in their lives. When an individual, such as Angela (whose case is discussed below), has both high levels of physical tension and chronic pain, the tension may further increase the pain, and the pain will cause even more tension in the muscles. EMT can break this cycle.

In her late forties and happily married with two successful adult children, Angela was plagued with severe headaches, and chronic backache and neck ache, related to many years of repetitive muscle strains from bending and lifting work. Through the EMT intervention (fingertaps), it became clear that physical tension was contributing to her pain. The tap-induced relaxation was effective in reducing her tension to a low level. Because focusing on her pain and stress did not produce any relief, she was asked to focus on the phrase "relax," *ree* when she inhaled and *laaax* when she exhaled, as the EMT procedure was done. This combination of EMT and breathing focus produced a sleep-like relaxation, although her neck continued to hurt. Over the next three rounds of EMT taps, she felt like she was being drained of stress and experienced a mild euphoria. The release of tension was experienced as heat coming out her shoulders. The pain lessened and the tight, tense feelings subsided.

The fingertap relaxation was effective in reducing Angela's tension from a 9 to a 3 (0 being no tension) in about five minutes. The pain eased somewhat and was more tolerable. Home practice of EMT for relaxation induced a more restful sleep. At a follow-up visit two weeks later, Angela reported successful relaxation with EMT, fewer pain-related awakenings during the night, and a feeling of improved restfulness when she woke up in the morning.

Headache Relief with EMT

Severe, persistent headaches, including migraine, tension, and cluster headaches, may be triggered and intensified by stress. Of course, other factors contribute to these headaches, including hereditary factors, hormonal influences, drug and alcohol consumption, and diet. According to a recent survey of migraine sufferers, 50 percent of the respondents believed that stress played an important role in their headaches. In my clinical experience, anger and worry are the predominant emotions that contribute to debilitating headaches. The anger may be directed at others or at yourself and the worry is often quite generalized. A fair number of headache suffers, especially migraineurs, say that they are "worrywarts."

Once again, the stress-pain connection can be identified through EMT for people with chronic headache. Then the headache-related stress and tension can be relieved. The benefit to you will be: fewer headaches, of less severity and shorter duration. Once the stress factor is controlled, you will have eliminated at least one important headache trigger.

Treating Headaches: Migraine and Tension-Type

The two individuals discussed below suffered from both migraine and tension headaches. Their headaches were severe, and sometimes disabling. Both of them had tried numerous prescribed and over-the-counter drugs with little effect.

Sandra reported a history of migraine and tension headaches related to stress, as well as diet. The stress factors in her life included a sixteen-year-old son with poor grades, a husband with (treatable) cancer, and the responsibility of three part-time jobs. She also felt depressed about her persistent headaches. It was possible that her tension helped to trigger her headaches or that the headaches may have caused her to feel tense and depressed. Or it could have been both processes at work in a cycle. The EMT helped to identify these interactions.

The first EMT series diverted Sandra's attention from her headache to her breathing. Her head almost stopped hurting. But the headache came right back once the EMT tapping stopped. In the next EMT, she was asked to focus on the headache itself rather than her breathing. This strategy alleviated the headache on one side of her head. Then she focused on the one-sided headache as the next EMT was done. To her surprise, the headache disappeared. She also realized that her sullen mood was gone. Of course, this suggested that she had been depressed about her headache, rather than other things in her life. The EMT revealed two ways for Sandra to approach the headache: If focusing on her breathing did not help, then she should focus on the headache itself.

Using the EMT technique at home, Sandra was able to reduce the frequency and duration of her headaches over the next two months, at which point treatment was terminated.

Jeffrey, a thirty-two-year-old insurance adjuster, also suffered from severe migraine and tension headaches. He lost three or four working days a month due to the disabling effects of these headaches. When his headaches were severe, he had to lay in bed in a darkened, quiet room. EMT taps were initially given to generate and deepen feelings of relaxation for Jeffrey. The goal was to counteract the physical and emotional tensions that were contributing to his headaches. At first, Jeffrey focused on the feeling of physical tension in his body while I did the taps. The result: He was distracted from the headache and felt more relaxed. At one point, about a minute after the taps had started, he felt a pleasant waving motion through his eyelids, and thought he might fall asleep.

After the next series of EMT taps he looked surprised and relieved, and said: "With the tapping, I feel like I'm apart from my body. It distracts me from the pain in my neck and the pressure in my eyes. It also distracts me from having other thoughts. Just as you stopped the tapping, I felt like I was floating a bit. I mean, it's a bit startling. You don't feel the rest of your body so much. I felt a pleasant, wavy sensation across my face. Subtle, but still a sensation. Most of the time I have weird sensations associated with the headache, but this one, at least, wasn't painful. My whole body became loose, in effect."

Now, if Jeffrey could reproduce these feelings on his own, it would help him to alleviate his headaches. Less tension and more relaxation is usually associated with less headache. A one-month follow-up confirmed that Jeffrey was able to do the EMT taps himself and to create the floating, wavy feelings of relaxation. About 50 percent of the time, he reduced the severity of his debilitating headaches without medication. During the month, he missed only one day of work, rather than the usual three or four. Also, for the first time, he could control the headaches himself rather than depending on medications that often did not work.

Private Time and Pain Control

For people with chronic pain, severe pain flare-ups are sometimes best handled in private. Yet it is often difficult to break away from family or job obligations. EMT can help you assert your right to have time alone to cope with pain flare-ups.

Although John enjoyed spending time with his wife and two-and-a-half-year-old daughter, he wanted to strengthen his ability to assert himself with family and friends when he needed a "pain break." Unfortunately, his chronic headaches interfered with his enjoyment of his family. Even the stress of ordinary social interactions eventually increased the severity of his headache. A brief period of downtime by himself could lessen the pain and allow him to return to normal activities with family and friends, but John was usually hesitant to ask for his time.

For John, EMT relaxed his body and reinforced his coping and assertive skills. The session started with John imagining being with his family and friends while a headache developed. The EMT helped to bolster his assertiveness: He imagined telling them that he had to take the break. He thought of their understanding, tolerant reactions to his need to take "pain breaks." John knew that to alleviate the pain, he needed time to fully relax in a quiet room. If he could reduce his pain from an intolerable level (10 on a 0 to 10 scale) to a more manageable level (about a 5), then he could return to the social gathering and enjoy it. Two more EMT procedures strengthened his motivation to handle social situations in such a way that he could spend as much time as possible with family or friends without being disabled by a headache. A six-month follow-up showed that he was continuing to use the relaxation and EMT on himself to lessen pain and reinforce his assertive right to ease pain-related stress in seclusion.

Stopping a Headache Early

Relaxation for headache control is a well-established and documented procedure. EMT can be used exclusively as a relaxation technique apart from its ability to resolve stress and conflict. The advantage of EMT-induced relaxation is that it is extremely rapid and long lasting. This fact is very important for the chronic headache sufferer who must catch the headache early, with either a behavioral technique or medication, to have any dampening effect on the full-blown headache.

Tess, age twenty-seven, suffered severe migraines that prevented her from working as a guidance counselor for one day every other week. With her strong work ethic, it was very annoying to her to miss work for any reason. She was also concerned about unsatisfactory work evaluations due to her absences.

Tess's migraines were related to a sometimes overwhelming fear that when she felt a sensation of pressure in the back of her head, she would develop a debilitating headache (which often happened). During the session, she began to feel that anticipatory pressure sensation. At this point, I intervened with the EMT in an effort to block the potentially severe headache. An excerpt of the session illustrates how the EMT was used.

Tess: The discomfort is getting worse. I feel a pressure in the back of my head.

Therapist: I'd like you to focus on that pressure in the back of your head and we will continue. [EMT.] Let your eyes open, and what's happening now?

Tess:	I've just been thinking: I hope the head pressure doesn't get bad. I'm really afraid of that. I'm afraid of pain like that. That's what I was thinking now. Because I do feel a little bit of pain over here and a tiny little bit over here, and I just don't want it to get worse.
Therapist:	When you get afraid of an oncoming headache, it fuels more stress into your system, and it may contribute to the severity of the headache. Focus on that fear of getting a headache, just the fear itself. Do you think you could do that? Here we go. [EMT.] Let your eyes open, and what's happening now?
Tess:	The fear of the headache is still there.
Therapist:	Okay. Let's do a relaxation technique. What I would like you to do is focus on the word *relax*. Think *ree* as you inhale and *laaax* as you exhale, while I do the taps. I would like to calm you down. You are getting immersed in your fear of a headache. So the thing to do now is get away from it. Think *reee* as you inhale, *laaax* as you exhale. [EMT.] And what's happening now?
Tess:	Easing up some.
Therapist:	You were able to say the *relax* phrase?
Tess:	Yes.
Therapist:	Sounds good. Let's continue with the *relax* phase. [EMT.] Let your eyes open, and what's happening now?
Tess:	I'm feeling calmer.
Therapist:	Where are you, 0 to 10 on the stress scale, right now.
Tess:	A 3.
Therapist:	Very good. Okay. Notice that you got to the brink of a headache, but then you stopped the worry and relaxed yourself, which is something you can do on your own. Instead of the fear taking over and immediately taking a shot [medication injection] for the migraine headache, you can calm yourself down and get rid of those early headache signals. Try this on your own, and you can avoid some of your headaches.

In the subsequent weeks, Tess became much more aware of her fear reactions to an oncoming headache. Rather than running to the medicine cabinet for a headache remedy, which didn't always work, she sat in a comfortable chair and did the EMT relaxation. As a result, she developed confidence about controlling her headaches, rather than feeling victimized by them. In the month following the EMT visit, she did not miss a single day of work.

Alleviating Morning Pain

Taking the edge off of chronic pain when it is severe may be just the boost you need to persevere through a difficult day. Jackie, at fifty-one, had a long history of chronic jaw, neck, and abdominal pain. Medications for pain had minimal effect. The persistent pain had caused her to stop working as a nurse, and she was emotionally distressed by pain flare-ups. The most severe pain occurred upon awakening in the morning.

In a therapy session, she was given a hand tap EMT procedure as she focused on her breathing. The EMT relaxation produced a lessening of tension in about one minute. The hand taps were then given for shoulder and neck pain, which produced a significant reduction of these pains. Finally, she was taught to do knee taps on herself which resulted in a further release of tension. I prescribed the knee taps for home use in the morning when her pain was especially severe.

Over the following six months, Jackie routinely used the knee taps in the morning for pain. She thought to herself, "It's not so bad," while she did the knee taps to herself. The result: increased relaxation and better pain tolerance. She functioned around the house with much greater ease and comfort. Most importantly, Jackie was considering a return to nursing part-time to test her newly acquired ability to cope with persistent pain.

Relief from Diabetic Pain

Patricia walked into my office with an agonized expression on her face. She was demoralized about her diabetic neuropathy, a deterioration of the nerve endings in the hands and feet which caused her moderate to severe pain. If you can imagine walking with hot, burning sensations on the soles of your feet, then you can begin to understand her frustration and discouragement. Not only was her mobility greatly reduced, pain in her hands would flare whenever she picked up an object or even brushed against a nappy towel. Yet Patricia was not generally dissatisfied with her life. She had a happy marriage of twenty-one years with five children, ages four to sixteen. However, because of the pain condition, she had been unable to work for the past three years.

From this description, you might think that her pain was a purely physical response to a chronic, disabling disease. How could EMT really help her, a technique that reduces stress and changes thinking? Patricia discovered through EMT and general relaxation techniques that her personal feelings of stress, anxiety, and worry were, indeed, contributing to her pain. During the first EMT series, in which I tapped her knees because her hands were in pain, the pain in her extremities declined from a 7 to a 1. This improvement indicated that her extremity pain was almost eliminated. She was dumbstruck by this quick improvement.

We further discovered that she was worried about future pain flare-ups and the miserable life she would have with her pain. As these worries were significantly eased during the next EMT, she viewed the prospect of future pain as more manageable. After the session, Patricia used the EMT plus general relaxation techniques to sustain calm feelings throughout the day. As a result, her ability to use her hands and walk greater distances improved.

At her last visit, Patricia reported spending several hours shopping at a local mall with her husband, and they had a thoroughly enjoyable day. By comparison, she had not been able to walk for more than a half hour at a time for the past three years. Her pain severity was cut roughly in half. The EMT helped her to manage her stress in general and her worry about the pain, in particular. The salutary effects of EMT on this individual once again demonstrate the importance of stress in the experience of persistent pain.

Easing the Pain of Arthritis

Angela, a sixty-six-year-old retired school teacher, had a number of medical problems, including arthritis pain and depression. Although she wanted to enjoy hobbies and activities, her pain, fatigue, and depression interfered with her enjoyment and left her nearly immobilized. A previously undiagnosed thyroid problem was successfully treated with medication, which improved her energy, and an antidepressant medication relieved her depression. Yet no medication was successful in reducing her arthritic pain or her persistent worry about becoming completely disabled as a result of her medical problems.

The key question: How much did psychological stress in the form of worry and frustration increase her arthritic pain? She was not aware of any such connection, and because she was almost continually stressed, it was difficult to draw a relationship between pain and stress. To address the issue, I did an initial round of EMT taps while she focused on her frustration and worry about the pain and its possible disabling consequences. She rated the pain and stress at a 7 to 8 level (out of a possible 10). The pain was most intense in her right knee.

After only three minutes of taps, she laughed, opened her eyes, and said: "It's working. My knee is feeling better." Angela was quite surprised that stress could influence her pain so strongly. She now remarked that she had to become more aware of stress and how it was affecting her pain. Another round of taps reduced her pain further, to a low level of 3. She was given a home assignment, to do the taps when her pain flared, which would probably mean that her stress had increased as well.

Reducing Fibromyalgic Pain

Fibromyalgia is a commonly reported, yet poorly understood, chronic pain condition that afflicts mostly women. Affected individuals experience widespread pain, often in the legs, shoulders, and neck. The pain itself can be disabling, while other symptoms, including persistent fatigue, headaches, sleep disturbance, and memory and concentration problems contribute to the overall severity of the illness. The causes of fibromyalgia are unknown and no cure or effective treatment is yet available.

Patty, age twenty-three, had been ill with fibromyalgia and chronic fatigue for four years. Prior to becoming ill, she had led a very active lifestyle, which included full-time work at a film studio and daily aerobic exercise. But over a period of only a few days, she became very ill and experienced severe leg pain that interfered with walking and moving about. Sometimes the pain was so intense that she had to crawl. The illness caused her so much stress that she modestly hoped for an occasional good day when she could feel somewhat better and do more.

As Patty was most debilitated by the pain in her legs, I decided to use the EMT as a potential treatment for her leg pain. After the first series of taps, she felt relaxed and almost sleepy, but the leg pain was still very strong. After the second series of taps, she was amazed to report that the leg pain had eased considerably. Two further rounds of taps reduced the pain from a high of 10 to a 0, or no pain.

It seems that Patty did not realize how much the stress of being ill had affected her. This ongoing stress may have been one reason why her leg pain remained as severe as it was. She was assigned the taps for home use. Two weeks later she reported that the taps reduced the leg pain to 0 for about fifteen minutes, after which the pain would remain at a low level for several hours. This striking result was achieved with two to three minutes of taps.

I cannot say that the taps always work so well for fibromyalgic pain, but given the high levels of stress that most people report with fibromyalgia, it is likely that EMT can reduce this stress and any pain that may be triggered by it.

Easing Symptoms of Chronic Fatigue Syndrome

Chronic pain is often accompanied by feelings of persistent fatigue. When chronic fatigue begins suddenly with disabling symptoms, it may become an illness in its own right. Chronic fatigue syndrome (CFS) is a debilitating condition whose major symptoms include severe, persistent fatigue, inability to exercise, sleep disturbance, mental fogginess, joint or muscle pain, and a number of other disconcerting bodily sensations.

The cause or causes of CFS are unknown and no cure or effective treatment is available. However, the technique of EMT can help with the stress caused by the illness, as well as the CFS symptoms themselves. Any of the fatigue symptoms can be used as a target for EMT. Simply focus on the symptom you wish to ease and use the tap procedure. You will probably get a reduction in that particular symptom. I have successfully used the tap procedure on the mental fogginess that many people with CFS experience. This mental fogginess can be associated with other cognitive symptoms including difficulty concentrating, forgetfulness, inability to find words, or using words incorrectly.

One particular success story with EMT and CFS comes to mind. At fifty-eight, Steve had enjoyed excellent health all his life until eighteen months earlier when he began experiencing severe chronic fatigue. He was forced to give up his successful private law practice due to fatigue-related disability. His marriage of two years was strained due to his limitations, and he lost his sexual desire. Most disturbing to him were the cognitive problems of mental haziness, difficulty paying attention, and frequent forgetfulness.

In the session he was asked to focus on the mental haziness while I tapped the back of his hands. Over an eight-minute tapping session, he felt the haziness lifting, although it came back a few minutes later. With home practice of the tap procedure, he was successful in alleviating these sensations for one to two hours. This new found control over his cognitive symptoms provided Steve with hope that he could learn to cope better with the illness. Over a twelve-month period of rehabilitation, his illness gradually improved.

Stella, a thirty-seven-year-old woman who had had CFS for nine years, lost her job as a court reporter ten months previously. She could no longer perform her duties because of concentration difficulties, and the intrusive symptom of severe fatigue had recently intensified. The illness made her so stress-sensitive that ordinary reading could trigger a migraine headache and gastrointestinal distress.

Stella came to her first session seeking help with her concentration and memory problems. An initial breathing-focus relaxation technique (about fifteen minutes) helped her to relax from the chest downward; however, she still experienced significant tension and strain in her head, neck, and shoulders. Because the breathing-focus technique usually relaxes the entire body, her residual feelings of tension indicated a very high level of generalized stress.

I tried the EMT tapping technique as she focused on the stress in the back of her neck. After three rounds of tapping (about ten minutes), she discovered that she was telling herself over and over, "Nothing is going to work." Frustrated by this pessimistic thought, Stella forcefully tried to banish it from her mind. Predictably, her attempts to suppress the negative thought increased her feelings of tension. She now felt the early sensations of a developing headache.

Once this negative thought was identified as an obstacle to the success of the EMT, the obstacle itself became the focus of the technique. Rather than trying to fight off a negative thought, it can be controlled more easily by simply focusing on it. Ordinarily, Stella would think pessimistic thoughts *automatically* and then would rebuke herself for being pessimistic. Alternatively, she was now asked to *voluntarily* produce the negative thought. As a result, she was exerting more control over the negative thought by voluntarily focusing on it rather than being victimized by it throughout the day when it came unbidden. As she focused on the thought, I did another round of taps.

By the end of the taps she began to smile, and almost laugh. She now realized how silly the pessimistic thought was. Focusing on it, rather than trying to push it away, helped her to reach that conclusion. As the negative thought faded away, she felt a release in the tension in the back of her neck and her shoulders. This was a breakthrough for Stella, who had never realized how tense she was in that area until she could contrast it with the newly induced feeling of relaxation.

In subsequent sessions we found that Stella's high level of baseline tension was probably contributing to her frequent migraine headaches, and her symptoms of CFS as well. Therapy with Stella was later expanded to address important family and relationship issues that were related to her CFS. By the end of treatment, her ability to concentrate had returned, and she was able to resume working part-time as a court reporter.

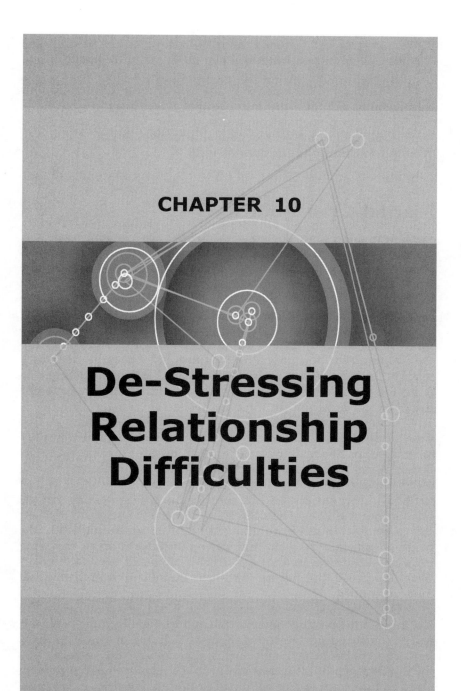

CHAPTER 10

De-Stressing Relationship Difficulties

This chapter will examine the role of stress on relationship and marital problems, including marital conflicts, separations and breakups, irrational jealousy, and sexual harassment at work. EMT can alleviate the emotional anguish of these crisis situations substantially, although the interpersonal issues may require more therapeutic work, such as couples counseling. When personal stress is reduced, your ability to examine and resolve important issues in your relationships will improve as well.

Marital Crisis and EMT

Jenna was angry and depressed about her deteriorating marriage. Only two and a half years into the marriage, her husband was becoming distant, and their sexual relationship had disappeared. And he seemed to have no inclination to repair the relationship. In the marital session with her husband present, it was clear that she spent an inordinate amount of time blaming him and literally pointed a finger at him as she said over and over, "You should do this, you shouldn't do that." One goal of marital counseling is to stop the blaming behavior, no matter how justified it may be, because it tends to further erode the marital relationship. But my suggestions to Jenna to stop the blaming were ignored, as she insisted that she had the right to blame him for what he had done wrong.

Although I was making no progress with Jenna, I could see that she was very tense and agitated in sessions, so I suggested an EMT tap procedure. She readily agreed to EMT, because she wanted to feel better, at least on an emotional level, if not in her marriage. During the procedure, she felt tension release from the entire upper half of her body. Then, she cried as she contemplated the possibility that the relationship was over. The EMT allowed her to consciously consider this previously suppressed thought. As her upset subsided, she began to generate more positive coping statements about surviving regardless of the future of the marriage. Jenna still wanted the marriage to succeed, but her more realistic outlook allowed her to feel more in control.

Over the next several sessions she remained calmer than she had been in the past two months. She reduced her blaming behavior, and her husband made greater efforts to help the marriage, perhaps in reaction to her behavioral changes. I cannot say with certainty that the EMT triggered this improvement in the relationship, but nothing else I had done up to that point had produced any change. My opinion is that the EMT did facilitate changes in her emotions and behavior that helped the marital counseling move forward. About six months later, I happened to encounter Jenna in a local shop. She smiled easily and appeared comfortable and relaxed. She was happy to tell me that her relationship with her husband had improved and that they were able to reconcile.

Getting Rid of Marital Anger

Don and Cynthia, a couple in their early forties with four-year-old twins, were angry at each other for many, many reasons. Cynthia's big complaint was her husband's self-righteous anger about the way she disciplined the kids. On the other hand, thought she was too permissive, allowing the kids to get "out of control" before she intervened. In general, Don tended to make soap box speeches about things that she did wrong and this infuriated her. Her second complaint was that Don was building a vacation house in Maine, several hours away, and had been gone for many weekends, leaving her and the kids alone. Although these absentee weekends had happened over a year and a half ago, she was still resentful about it. Finally, he had taken off an entire year from work two years ago, saying that it was a "sabbatical," and they had had to survive on their savings. This was another source of ongoing aggravation and resentment for Cynthia. In sum, she was in a perpetual state of annoyance about past issues as well as current problems.

For his part, Don complained about his wife's easygoing attitude toward the kids and was resentful that she was so close to her family and took advice from them but rarely from him. In his view, she spent all of her time with the kids and devoted little effort to their relationship.

The truth of the situation, as I saw it, was that Cynthia did spend too much time with the kids and was too fastidious with housecare. She did not work on the marital relationship or spend much time with her husband. And Don was focused on his personal interests, like building a vacation house and doing an hour and a half of vigorous exercise every day. He did not pay attention to problems with the kids. Instead, he somehow expected that the kids would act like little adults rather than playful, rambunctious children.

Through counseling, Don learned to walk away from situations that would trigger his explosive temper. His newfound ability to take timeouts resulted in fewer arguments; however, he remained angry about certain issues. On the other hand, Cynthia's anger remained unabated during the marital sessions. I scheduled individual sessions for each of them in order to teach the EMT tapping techniques. Cynthia focused on her anger about Don's righteous speech making, and within a few minutes her anger diminished to a low level. She said, "It's just not important that I listen to Don's speeches and react to them." This was an important new insight that I had previously thought she would never recognize or accept.

Don initially focused on his anger about Cynthia slamming the door around the house, which reminded him of his mother doing the same thing when he was a child. Once again, within a few minutes, his anger rapidly diminished and he said, "I feel relaxed. I don't have to react so emotionally to these little annoyances." He was also de-stressed to the angry thought of Cynthia going into another room of the house and cursing him in a low voice. This had upset him greatly in the past, but through the EMT tapping, he could think about it more calmly by telling himself, "She brought her anger problem to the marriage. I didn't create it."

They were both assigned the taps to do individually when they got angry. The couple struggled over several months to change their behavior and reduce their anger, and suffered many setbacks. After all, they were attempting to change lifelong patterns. Yet the arguing lessened, and their ability to cope with each other's annoying habits improved.

Marital Separations

Marital separations generate a panoply of stressful emotions including anger, fear, insecurity, guilt, depression, and worry. Bob's wife of fifteen years had left him two weeks previously to live in her own apartment. He was devastated by the event, but admitted to unjustly accusing her of infidelity for the past several years. She finally tired of his accusations and decided to leave. Feeling distraught, he had missed work for the past two days.

Bob's angry accusations were related to negative feelings about his physical appearance and weight. He traced these insecurities back to childhood when his parents favored his older brother, who treated Bob as a personal slave. With such a long history of apparent emotional battering, any experienced psychotherapist might reasonably predict that long-term counseling would be in order to change the emotional patterns that led to the destructive marital jealousy. Although I am not claiming that EMT will repair a damaged marriage, the rapid resolution of some of the emotional issues involved may allow the couple to make decisions about the marriage with less conflict and acrimony.

Bob's greatest fear was that his wife would divorce him. He felt a generalized dread about the future that triggered panicky feelings, nausea, and feelings of collapse. When he arrived in my office, he was desperate for any intervention that would help him cope with his misery. Anyone in Bob's position, receiving the unexpected shock of a marital separation and possible divorce, would be understandably upset. Support from family and friends might be helpful, but it probably would not alleviate the fear of a marital breakup. Likewise, talking therapy alone is less likely to be effective with a client who is consumed with fear and dread. Standard relaxation techniques could be helpful if the client could focus his attention on the therapist's calming suggestions during the procedure. In my eighteen years experience as a psychotherapist, I've found that such an intense emotional upheaval is often resistant to my best efforts to ease stress and generate good feelings. Because Bob was so severely distraught I decided to try EMT as a first approach to alleviating his anxiety. I have often seen EMT "compel" relaxation in people who are too upset to pay attention to relaxing suggestions or to feel encouraged by supportive comments.

EMT did indeed work rapidly for Bob. In only fifteen minutes, his fear and demoralization was replaced with deep relaxation and constructive thoughts about how his marriage could be saved. Most importantly, this brief EMT visit generated optimism to replace the deep despair about the separation. I believe that the immediate stress relief produced by the EMT was an important factor in facilitating his return to work.

Bob and his wife were able to reconcile over a twelve-month period with the assistance of marital counseling. Although I have seen EMT work rapidly with highly distressed people, I am not suggesting that it will work so well with everyone. Yet it often succeeds where standard approaches fail. When your stress level becomes unbearably intense, try the EMT technique. It may just give you the relief that you thought was not possible.

Easing the Anger Toward Your Spouse

John had been married thirteen years and had an eleven-year-old daughter. Over the past few years of his marriage, he had been working sixty to seventy hours per week as a corporate attorney. At home, he was exhausted and had little time or energy to spend with his wife and daughter. He seemed to turn a blind eye to their protests about his lack of involvement and thought that the marriage was "okay." After all, he *had* to work to support the family. The marriage was slowly coming apart, but he did not want to recognize it or face the problems. When his wife began working outside of the home, he became suspicious about her late hours and accused her of having an affair, which she angrily denied. In a few weeks' time, these confrontations escalated to nasty, name-calling arguments. Finally, she insisted on a six-month separation, which John reluctantly agreed to.

Devastated by this sad turn of events, he sought counseling and began to realize his role in the unraveling of the marriage. He was extremely resentful about the lack of communication with his wife and blamed her for acting so precipitously with the separation. Because his anger was resistant to all of my efforts to diffuse it, I opted for the technique that often works with such tough customers: EMT.

As John focused on his resentment, I began the EMT technique. At first he felt distracted from his resentment and more relaxed. Although his resentment diminished during the first few minutes, he stopped my tapping and declared, "I should feel resentful, otherwise I'm giving in to her and then I'm the bad guy." It seemed he needed to feel angry to believe that he was right and good. He had not realized that previously. Without his anger, he would have to recognize the role he played in creating the marital problems. Clearly, this was an uncomfortable thought for him.

These new insights made him realize that any possibility of reconciliation required that he accept his share of the responsibility for creating the conflict in his marriage. As these new insights took hold and further EMT taps were done, his anger lessened to a very mild level. Through EMT, John made significant gains in insight, anger control, and his problems with intimacy. Unfortunately, it was too late to save his marriage, although he worked out a mutually agreeable settlement with his wife so they could continue to share parenting responsibilities.

Gaining the Courage to Break Up

Darren, a thirty-six-year-old attorney, had been divorced for two years from his wife and had an eight-year-old daughter. He was considering, but did not feel ready, to break up with Ellen, his girlfriend of one year who viewed the relationship as a temporary

"Band-Aid" for her failed marriage. Although Ellen was losing interest in him, Darren felt that he could not let go of her, and agreed with the therapist's term that he was "addicted" to the relationship. The word "addicted" jolted him into recognizing the unhealthy dependency he had on her. However, he felt that without her, he would never recapture the feelings created by the brief but very passionate affair they initially had.

The EMT helped Darren to reevaluate the worsening relationship, and to prepare to end it. At the beginning of the session, he focused on the thought that he would be "lost" without her. The EMT helped him to fully recognize how rarely Ellen reciprocated his feelings, something he could never acknowledge for more than a few seconds. He began to concede, reluctantly, that infatuation might describe the relationship better than love.

The EMT helped further to reveal his denial of the negative aspects of the relationship: Because he wanted to be Ellen's savior, he accommodated all of her requests and demands, but was afraid to ask for anything in return. The therapist commented, "And then what do you get for rescuing her? Unless you want to be Mother Teresa, you don't get very much for that. Not many people in this world will give one way and expect absolutely nothing in return, and by return I don't mean a slap in the face."

Over the next several weeks, Darren was given EMT while he focused on his girlfriend's indifference. As a result, he began to weigh the passionate sexual encounters against the neglect and rejection that he would suffer from seeing her again. Now the possibilities of a new, healthier relationship seemed more and more desirable. Significantly, he began to think that he did not have to prove himself constantly to a woman in order to be worthy of her.

After the Breakup, How to Stop Thinking About It

The breakup of a romantic relationship is often a wrenching emotional experience. Even if your feelings toward the person have diminished considerably, you may dwell on the dissolved relationship for weeks or months afterward and feel charged with negative emotions such as hurt, anger, jealousy, or guilt. The advice you get will usually be "time heals." Time usually does heal, but you don't need to suffer with these painful emotions as long as you may think.

EMT will hasten your emotional recovery from a failed relationship, lessen the intrusiveness of painful memories, and put them to rest more quickly. I would advise using EMT several times a day over a two- to three-week period to lessen painful ruminations about a past relationship. This requires only eight to ten minutes of EMT daily. The rewards for your efforts will be significant. Not only will you feel a sense of relief from the emotional turmoil, your normal levels of concentration and follow-through on routine activities will return. Below is an example of post-relationship stress and how it was substantially resolved in one EMT visit.

Michael, age thirty-nine, thought a lot about his ex-girlfriend, Chris, who had treated him poorly, saw him rarely, and had another boyfriend to boot. Even though his feelings for her were diminishing, he was stressed by memories of the relationship. He also feared that she would approach his new girlfriend, Linda, and attempt to undermine their relationship. The EMT focused on the intrusive thoughts about his ex. During the EMT, Michael also identified a knot in his chest associated with the emotional turmoil.

Michael used the EMT on himself, outside of therapy, on a daily basis to refocus his thinking on his current relationship and resolve the stress about the past, destructive relationship. Over a two-week period, he reported a dramatic lessening of his thoughts about the old relationship and a renewed energy and confidence in his ability to sustain his new, healthier involvement. He was able to keep his thoughts in the present rather than dwelling on his old relationship.

Jealousy and Suspicion

Jealousy, suspicion, and mistrust of your partner or spouse are destructive emotions that can undermine your relationship. I'm speaking of the type of jealousy that is irrational and unfounded, the type of jealousy that is intense and enduring despite the absence of any evidence of partner betrayal. In its extreme form, a person might fear that his or her partner is exposed to irresistible temptation just by leaving the house or by talking to someone of the opposite sex for any reason, no matter how innocent.

Jealousy torments the individual who experiences it. The feeling arises from the jealous partner's conviction that he or she is unworthy of his or her mate. The jealous person wonders: "Why does my partner stay with me?" With such self-doubt, you are more likely to believe that your partner would be tempted by any opportunity to hook up with someone else. Apart from the self-esteem issue, you may also think in a very possessive way about your partner, believing that your partner's thoughts and feelings should only focus on you. Although these possessive feelings seem highly irrational, they are not all that uncommon. You may recognize the absurdity of these types of thoughts, and yet not be able to control or banish them. I have used EMT for unfounded jealousy with very good results.

In her mid-twenties, Robin experienced an irrational jealousy that her husband would have a sexual encounter with his ex-girlfriend who lived across town. Although Robin had been married only eighteen months, she could not rid herself of these feelings of mistrust. Yet, during the initial EMT, she could not generate the intense jealousy (or even mild jealousy) that she normally experienced. She looked somewhat bewildered. After briefly pondering her sudden tranquillity, she now thought of the jealousy as being "silly" and "unnecessary." Of course, it was hard to tell how much she believed these new evaluations until she actually tested them the next time she felt suspicious toward her husband. I suggested that she practice these new beliefs when she got upset about the idea that her husband might visit the ex-girlfriend (which he had not done). If she could internalize these helpful ideas, that her unfounded fears were "silly" and "unnecessary," she might be less upset about the ex-girlfriend.

Robin's session illustrated an interesting variation on what can happen in an EMT visit. Some individuals cannot reexperience during the session the upset that they normally have had about their problem. Sometimes the EMT will not work because the stress cannot be recreated and used as a target for the technique. However, what can happen, and did, in the above session is that the thoughts of suspicion were reevaluated as "silly" *because* Robin could not get upset thinking about them. (Attempting to produce jealous or other stressful thoughts *voluntarily*, rather then automatically thinking the stressful thoughts without effort, may assist you in gaining control over the stressful thinking.) Also, the EMT did produce general relaxation, which may have helped Robin to rethink her unfounded suspicions and minimize their importance.

Sexual Harassment and Assertiveness

Sexual harassment involves uninvited and unwanted sexual remarks, sexual behavior, or physical contact. When it happens, many women (and men) do not know how to handle it effectively. Often the person who is harassed in a work setting feels offended and angry but may feel (understandably) inhibited about confronting the person, who may be a boss or supervisor.

Carol, age thirty-nine, was happily married for nineteen years with two teenage children. Although her part-time nursing job was satisfying to her, she was extremely sensitive to criticism in her work setting and feared speaking up for herself, thinking that people would never speak to her again. She wanted to be more assertive but thought it would be nearly impossible to change her behavior. At the time I began treating Carol, her nonassertive behavior had made her the target of more than occasional criticism—she was the victim of offensive sexual innuendoes directed toward her by a male coworker. She felt insulted by his comments, and tried to ignore him, but he continued to taunt her. She didn't know what else to do. Carol suffered stress headaches from these encounters, yet was afraid to express her objections, fearing that the coworker would never talk to her again. She rated the stress as an 8 on a 0 to 10 scale. The EMT session proceeded as follows:

Therapist: Now, I would like you to imagine your coworker never talking to you again. Can you think about it and generate that fear? Okay. By speaking up, you fear being a troublemaker and losing his friendship. Can you imagine him making the sexual remarks and you wanting to object? Good. Let your eyes close. [EMT hand taps begin, but Carol grasps the therapist's hands after about fifty taps to stop the procedure.] You seem annoyed. Why?

Carol: Tapping my hands. Stop it!

Therapist: Okay. What makes that annoying to you, do you know?

Carol: It's annoying.

Therapist: Were you thinking about anything else?

Carol: [In a raised voice.] Yeah, stop it!

Therapist: Does this remind you of something that you don't like?

Carol: This guy talking to me like that. I mean, stop it!

Therapist: I take it that my tapping your hands had extra meaning for you? It was like an invasion of privacy.

Carol: Yeah. Without my permission, you kept doing it.

Therapist: Okay. But I did tell you I was going to do the taps.

Carol: Right, but enough is enough.

Therapist: Well, we are on to something here. You did say "stop it," and I stopped. If you said that, just that loud, to this guy when he makes the unwanted sexual remarks, he would stop. Now, I would like to continue with the EMT, not with the taps, since I know you have a negative feeling about it. We are going to do the eye movement this time. Focus on my hand. [EMT eye movement.] What's happening now?

Carol: I don't like this eye movement.

Therapist: The eye movement also seems to bug you. You know why?

Carol: No.

Therapist: I think it's the idea that I am controlling you somehow.

Carol: Right.

Therapist: And you feel controlled in so many ways by other people. So you rebelled against it here in the session. There is a way around this problem. I can teach you how to do the taps to yourself, right now. Okay. Put your hands on your lap, let your eyes close, and think about this guy talking to you. Do you have it?

Carol: Yes.

Therapist: I want you to move your index fingers up and down on your thighs. Left and right, one at a time. That's it, keep alternating, a little faster. Now think about the coworker making remarks. [EMT self-taps.] What is happening now?

Carol: I feel anger about him. I want to punch him in the face. If he was right in front of me, I would tell him off.

Therapist: So the emotional issue is unfolding. The intense anger is directed toward him. How is it doing the taps on your own?

Carol: Good.

Therapist: You are controlling the technique now, that's the way you like it. Do you want to continue with this?

Carol:	Sure.
Therapist:	Okay. Think about the anger. [EMT.] What is happening now?
Carol:	Feel tired.
Therapist:	Okay. It is draining, all of the anger coming to the surface. Your anger has probably been pent up for weeks. Now, how are you viewing this situation with this guy at work?
Carol:	I have to stop him.
Therapist:	How are you going to do that?
Carol:	By telling him forcefully, "Cut it out."
Therapist:	How do you feel about doing that?
Carol:	Better.
Therapist:	What if he never talks to you again?
Carol:	Oh, he'll talk to me.
Therapist:	You are pretty sure of that?
Carol:	I'm pretty sure of that now. He has no other choice, he works with me.
Therapist:	So to think he will never talk to you again is just unrealistic. He will talk to you. How about your feelings of being insulted? Do you feel it now?
Carol:	It's a little better. Like you said, it's up to me to stop him.

By the end of this very brief, ten-minute EMT session, Carol felt confident that she could just say in a loud voice, "Stop it!" There was no fear of the coworker not talking to her afterward. Interestingly, the taps on the back of the hand felt intrusive to her. Even that form of contact was experienced by her as an unwanted physical intrusion from the therapist. The eye movement, as well, generated a feeling that the therapist was trying to control her. It was as if the therapist had become simply another male who was imposing on her. When she did the self-taps, however, she did make progress, feeling that she was in control. Two weeks later, when the coworker resumed making the sexual remarks, she loudly told him to stop. She had no further trouble with him.

CHAPTER 11

Managing
Family Problems

Parenting Issues

On television, life seems so easy—perfect children and parents who can solve any problems with humor in half an hour or less. But real life is a different story. Parents' concerns about how to deal with their children bring many families to the therapist's door. Common parenting concerns include difficulty communicating with their children, issues of love and respect, problems with discipline, academic performance and homework, peer relationships in their children's lives, and differences in parenting style between father and mother. The last issue, conflicts over parenting style, is the subject of the EMT session below.

Different Parenting Styles

Andrea, age forty-three, was angry at her three kids about their sloppy habits and laziness. When this anger was used as the target of the initial EMT, Andrea's core emotions were revealed: anger about her husband's lax parenting of their kids and worry about her children's future. The EMT session virtually resolved these conflicts in twenty-five minutes.

Therapist: Okay. Think about your worst fears: your kids having no friends and just staying home and watching television. As you just described to me, that's quite a stressful image to contemplate. It triggers intense worry. Can you get this idea in mind? You're sitting home on the weekends and all of these worrisome thoughts become overwhelming. Do you have the image?

Andrea: Yes. It's becoming very clear, and I feel the stress as well.

Therapist: All right, I will begin the EMT by tapping your hands. Now during the tapping, the image may change or it may stay the same. It's hard to predict. Things may start to feel more stressful, or less stressful. There's no rule on how it should go. I will ask you specifically what your thoughts and feelings are after each series. The ultimate goal is to have you feel less stressed. Now, let your eyes close. [EMT.] Okay. Let your eyes open, and what is happening now?

Andrea: I was visualizing the kids in their pajamas. Me trying to get them moving and then the kids getting madder at me than they ever do at my husband. You know, my husband can yell at them and they never seem to get angry at him or show disrespect.

Therapist: And why do they get mad at you?

Andrea: If I just ask them to do anything. If we both yell at them separately for the same thing, they would cool off afterward and talk to Bill, my husband, in about five minutes, but they would just stay mad at me.

Therapist: Okay. Let's continue with the image you're getting now about your kids and your husband. [EMT.] What's happening now?

Andrea: I was focusing on Jimmy, my son. He yells. I mean he just has a loud mouth. A few times when I've said something and he's yelled back, I've gotten very upset. And my husband's reaction would be, "Yes, he shouldn't yell at you. Yes, I'll talk to him about it." But he'll then say, "You have to realize that he is only fourteen years old and not to take it so personally." So I was focusing on that, and that helped. If he answers back, then I have to realize that rather than seeing it as disrespect, he may be seeing it as asserting his right to independence.

Therapist: Focus on that [the previous sentence]. [EMT.] What's happening now?

Andrea: Another related thing has come up that bugs me. I wash the clothes, put them away, but my son doesn't wear them, doesn't hang them up, and doesn't throw them in the wash. This really upsets me and when I say something to him, we have a conflict. But now I'm looking at it somewhat differently. I'm saying to myself not to even look in the wash. Let my husband take care of it. Let him retrieve the clean clothes and hang them up. I'm surprised I can even think that way.

Therapist: This idea of how to cope with the conflict over the clothes washing. Is this something you've thought of before?

Andrea:	I've fleetingly thought of it before, but I can't seem to believe it. I can't seem to let go of the idea that I have to insist on my son taking care of his clothes.
Therapist:	Okay. Focus on that. "I insist on getting into a squabble with my son." Just focus on that. Don't try to be constructive. [EMT.] What's happening now?
Andrea:	I'm imagining Jimmy graduating from high school and not going to college, not getting a job, sleeping all day. Tracy, my daughter, ending up in a bad school situation, getting in with bad people, dressing badly, getting pregnant, all those horrible things. That was bad.
Therapist:	Did that type of image raise your stress level?
Andrea:	Yes.
Therapist:	Continue thinking about it. [EMT.] What's happening now?
Andrea:	It got even worse. I took it to the point where the kids are in the house with all of these problems, and I just couldn't take it. I had to leave the house. I would blame my husband if he allowed them to live in this situation, you know. I wouldn't have the authority to control the direction of the kids. That's the bad part. So I feel like I would blame him because he didn't take on the authority role, which he could do.
Therapist:	Let me fashion a coping statement from what you've just said. Your husband is a fallible human being and father. He has the right to do not such a good job by the kids. He doesn't have to do the right thing, even though you wish he would. How does that sound?
Andrea:	Meaning that how they turn out is largely out of his hands too?
Therapist:	I think that is true. But I also think that even if he does the wrong thing, your insistence that he shouldn't is an impossible demand you place on him. So to diffuse your angry demand, you could tell yourself, "I don't like it, but he has the right to do it even if I don't like it."
Andrea:	And then what?

Therapist: Well, if you believe that, your anger will diminish and that's a large part of the stress you are feeling. Could you focus on that, "I don't like it, but he has the right to do it. How the kids turn out is largely up to them," which is true. Here we go. [EMT.] What's happening now?

Andrea: I feel better because I told myself whatever feelings my husband has, they are not out of any kind of meanness or malevolence toward the kids. He does try to set a good example. They never do see him doing morally wrong things, so if he makes mistakes, so what? The kids should look up to him even if, day to day, he does make mistakes and doesn't do everything right. I think of my parents, who did everything wrong, and I didn't turn out to be a failure. I have a very strong sense of right and wrong.

Therapist: That's true. You know there are studies comparing how kids turn out who have been brought up in orphanages versus ordinary, nuclear families. There isn't much of a difference in their adjustment as adults. So there is a very strong genetic push toward a certain type of adjustment in life. Parents only have limited influence over their children's success as adults.

Andrea: Yeah, I believe that. That's very interesting.

Therapist: Could you rate your stress level now, 0 to 10, about your kids not listening and your husband not intervening in their discipline.

Andrea: I would rate it about a 3.

Therapist: Have you ever felt so little stress about this issue?

Andrea: No, never. I'm really quite surprised.

Andrea remained in therapy for another month. By the end of that month, she had not experienced a flare-up of the anger and worry about her kids' future, their lack of compliance with her demands, or her husband's hands-off attitude about the kids' behavior. Clearly, the success of this session was a combination of the EMT technique freeing Andrea to identify the full scope of the problem and a possible resolution to it, as well as the generation of stress-reducing coping statements based on the principles of rational-emotive behavior therapy (Ellis 1973).

Easing Parenting Anger and Frustration

The difficulties of parenting in combination with other stressors, including work, marital, and financial concerns, can become overwhelming at times. Children, at certain ages, are naturally oppositional to their parents, and their ability to exercise self-control is, of course, limited by their immaturity.

Nicole, age thirty-seven, was concerned about her twelve-year-old, hyperactive daughter, Mae. She was frustrated and angry about Mae's temper tantrums and did not now how to handle them. Through the EMT, she recognized how angry she was at herself, because she felt helpless to stop her daughter's tantrums. Then she began to reevaluate her self-anger, which generated a relaxing thought: "I have the right to be frustrated with my daughter and myself." This more logical view lessened her self-anger and produced a visible calming in her demeanor. Rather than going head-to-head with Mae during a tantrum, she decided to take a few deep breaths, remember that she is the adult, and walk away until her daughter calmed down. She realized that Mae was very skilled at creating turmoil and drawing her into it. Nicole was demanding that her daughter should not bait her. She paused and said: "But I can't *make* her believe anything. I can't control her. She's her own person, and I'm beginning to think that maybe it's me wanting control. I don't have such control of my other kids—how can I have control over her?"

During the next EMT series, Nicole spontaneously imagined she was trying to give her pet bird a bath, and she associated the task with demanding that Mae stop an objectionable activity. She couldn't make the bird take the bath if it wasn't willing. Nor could she force her daughter to obey her. This mental juxtaposition made Nicole realize the futility and irrationality of many of her demands on her daughter. As a result, her anger diminished to a very low level.

At a one-month follow-up visit, Nicole reported that dealing with Mae was still difficult, but she was able to remove herself from the situation when her daughter started screaming uncontrollably. She used these new coping thoughts, "Mae has a right to overreact," and "I can walk away when she's acting out, calm myself, and then I can work better with her." Deep breaths helped her to regain control. Then she could talk to the girl when they were both calmer. As a result, there was less conflict and better communication between the two.

Boosting Your Self-Image After Pregnancy

Jeanine, age thirty-one, had gained 50 pounds during pregnancy. Prior to the pregnancy, she had carried a modest 110 pounds on her five-feet, two-inch frame. After the baby was born, she immediately shed 25 pounds, but then lost only four additional pounds over the next two months. This was most frustrating to her, because she was eating a nutritionally balanced 1,000 to 1,200 calories and walked a mile and a half each day. Jeanine was tempted to resume smoking after a year of abstinence, thinking that it might help her to lose weight. Although she resisted this unhealthy temptation, she was becoming completely demoralized by the stubborn weight problem.

The EMT focused on her weight-related stress and revealed a number of worries and concerns related to her appearance. She consciously thought of herself as the "picture of ugliness" and did not want to show herself publicly. Eventually the EMT relaxed her and made it more difficult to visualize herself as ugly. Then, she focused on the "slim me," as she called it, as the EMT proceeded. But this thought triggered yet another issue. Her mother and her in-laws had been telling her not to lose more weight because they felt she was healthier with the additional weight. They all said she looked wonderful. Jeanine felt patronized by their insistence that she looked fine when she knew that she didn't. Continuing the process of EMT in this session largely eradicated her annoyance about her family's comments. She then reassured herself that the continuing weight loss effort was healthy, as well as cosmetic.

With the issues of her public image and family pressures resolved another frustration revealed itself during the session. Three months after giving birth, Jeanine had not resumed a sexual relationship with her husband, although she had the desire and he was getting impatient. The doctor had recently approved the resumption of intercourse, but Jeanine felt self-conscious about her appearance. She could only imagine having sex in a darkened room that would hide her nudity. This was in contrast to her previous openness and enthusiasm about sex. Two more EMT series in this session reduced her stress about sexual intimacy to a low level. Despite her concerns about her appearance, she could "deal with it" when she was this relaxed. Although self-conscious, she was subsequently able to have sex with her husband and ultimately absorbed herself in the pleasant sensations and feelings.

This EMT session resolved Jeanne's problems in about twenty minutes. In my view, such a quick resolution of these significant issues—physical appearance and sexual responsiveness—would be highly unlikely in conventional psychotherapy.

A Parent's Guilt About Her Adult Daughter

Until about two decades ago, children routinely left their homes after high school or college. Jobs were plentiful and living costs were not out of line with entry level salaries. Today, however, the ability of the job market to pay a livable income for entry level positions has greatly diminished. Many young adults, discouraged by low salaries and the absence of gainful full-time jobs, are not leaving home or are returning home due to divorce, unemployment, or general dissatisfaction with living independently.

Diana, an accomplished professional musician at age fifty-nine, was plagued with anger, frustration, and worry about her thirty-six-year-old daughter's inability to get a job and become independent. The daughter, Erin, lived with Diana and her husband, and did as she pleased. Since childhood, when Erin was rarely disciplined, she had had a strong sense of entitlement and no sense of responsibility. These attitudes were not discouraged by Diana, even now. But Diana was aggravated about her daughter's lack of appreciation for all that was done for her. The initial EMT revealed a core of maternal guilt that was maintaining her endless tolerance of Erin's behavior.

Initially, Diana discovered that she still felt guilty about her lax parenting during her daughter's childhood some thirty-plus years ago. Although Diana's kids (a daughter and a son) always were well-provided for in a material sense, she wondered if they had been shortchanged emotionally because their father, a commercial ship captain, was usually away. Diana's guilt over her husband's absence became a convenient rationalization not to impose discipline on her kids. She sighed that Erin's low level of motivation as an adult had been reinforced by such permissive child rearing. Yet her son became a secure, confident adult, while her daughter was emotionally fragile.

Through the ongoing process of EMT in a single session, Diana began to reevaluate her guilt-producing thoughts, which yielded the following coping statements: "Why punish myself? Children are what they are. You can always imagine something you didn't do for your kids and feel guilty about it." These new ideas eased her guilt, but highlighted her anger about Erin's inactivity, which was so contrary to Diana's bustling and self-disciplined lifestyle. As often happens during EMT visits, unconscious aspects of a problem are revealed. Diana's personal revelation of intense guilt about how she had parented her daughter was significantly reduced with EMT-related relaxation and attitude change. With her guilt lessened and a new attitude in place, Diana could then discover and deal with her daughter. This session identified the full range of the problem and set the stage for Diana to rethink her beliefs about herself and her daughter.

After EMT, Diana insisted that Erin find full-time work and leave the house within six months. Four months later, her daughter left the house. Not surprisingly, their relationship improved. They could now have more mature mother-daughter interactions based on mutual love rather than an unhealthy dependency. A good counselor may have achieved this result without EMT, although I believe it would have required considerably more time to identify the unconscious feelings and motivations that were related to the presenting problem. The EMT opened up the most important and relevant issues with minimal time and effort.

A Father's Anger at His Wife and Daughter

Edward had been happily married for thirty years and had three grown children. Now retired at age seventy, he looked forward to leisurely days spent improving his home and yard, going fishing, and sharing more time with his wife. He liked his life to be organized and well-ordered. All of his large debts, including his house loan and car loan, were paid off. But he had been completely unaware that his wife had offered one of their credit cards to their twenty-eight-year-old daughter, who was in financial trouble. His daughter had a history of financial difficulties, so his wife's generous action was clearly a bad risk. When Edward discovered a $15,000 debt incurred by his daughter on their credit card statement, he was in shock.

He had worked twenty years as a firefighter and then another fifteen years as an insurance salesman. He just wanted to enjoy his retirement and have the financial means to do so. Yet it appeared that he was under an ominous cloud of potential credit problems if this debt was not paid off. He was angry at his wife for not telling him about the credit card loan and at his daughter for accumulating such a huge debt.

He came to the therapy sessions looking like he was ready to explode from aggravation at his wife and daughter. His wife would not discuss the problem with him, apparently because he got so angry when the subject was broached. Edward was desperate to talk to someone, if only to relieve his pent-up emotions. He saw no solution to this life-rattling burden. I first led Edward through a relaxation exercise, which calmed him somewhat. This was followed with an EMT tap procedure in which he focused on his anger and worry about the actions of his wife and daughter.

Edward began to reevaluate the situation in a stepwise fashion. He acknowledged that his daughter was keeping up with the minimum monthly payment, although he would have liked a quicker resolution of the debt. But, he conceded, "Incremental payments are better than none. It is not a catastrophe." He further recognized that his daughter was avoiding him because he was so angry. Yet he loved his daughter and wanted to restore their relationship. He also realized that his wife could not admit she was wrong about lending the credit card to their daughter. He acknowledged that his wife was somewhat of a crazy spender herself, so she had not instilled financial responsibility in their daughter.

At the next session, Edward said that he was now able to talk to his wife after three weeks of near silence between them over the issue. He felt more relaxed and had eliminated his anger and worry over the money. He could forgive his daughter. After a conversation with his wife, they agreed that any further loans or credit extensions to their daughter had to be mutually agreed upon. To restore the closeness with his wife, he took positive steps, including more compliments and physical affection, as she became more receptive to him.

Edward played a relaxation tape and used the EMT tap method several times a day to stay calm and better focused on his goals of forgiving his wife and daughter and accepting that he could not control the outstanding debt. Because he was a naturally keyed up and worried individual, he needed the daily stress reduction exercises to achieve this level of success. As a result, he reduced his daily tranquilizer pill to half the normal dosage.

Adult Children Dealing with Difficult Parents

Even as adult, sons and daughters may find themselves reenacting old parent-child relationships with their mature parents. For instance, adult children may respond to their parents with the same feelings of dependence and approval-seeking that they experienced as children. The two examples below show how adult children can learn to recognize these behaviors and then rethink their relationships with parents who have always been difficult.

Mother Embarrasses Me

Lynn, age thirty-one, was an outspoken yet very sensitive woman, who had had a stormy relationship with her mother since childhood. Her mother's unpredictable, nasty moods alternated with sudden crying spells that could be unnerving, as well as embarrassing. And she often imposed herself on Lynn with all kinds of unreasonable demands. When Lynn came to me for therapy, she was worried about her wedding, although it was still a year away. She anticipated the embarrassing things that her mother would say and do, as she often did in social gatherings. Feeling responsible for her mother's behavior in such situations, Lynn would attempt to explain away the dramatic outbursts and inappropriate remarks. She was afraid that people would think that she was nuts because of her mother's strange behavior.

During the first EMT series, she was initially successful in distancing herself from her mother's behavior by thinking along with the image of her mother, "It's okay. Say what you want, it doesn't really matter." However, during the second EMT series, Lynn became physically tense, her legs cramped, and she felt a tingling sensation throughout her body, especially in her jaw. She had had these symptoms on and off for many years. Her doctors had ruled out any medical condition, but she was not aware that stress might trigger these symptoms. Her physical tension and symptoms surfaced as she imagined her mother saying outlandish things at her wedding. For instance, her mother would easily get on the defensive in any conversation and sometimes say loudly, "I am who I am." Or, "I love God and God loves me." Or, "I'll sit next to God in heaven."

The next two EMT series suggested that Lynn was unconsciously attempting to deny and suppress her negative emotions related to her mother and the upcoming wedding. Instead of experiencing these emotions (anger and worry), she sensed only the physical symptoms and tension that were produced by these emotions. As she began to relax and then recognize the emotional blocking, she wondered why she suppressed emotional discomforts. Further EMT revealed an immense fear of losing control of her emotions and becoming like her mother. Lynn also realized that she never felt "worthy" to experience emotions, especially positive emotions. The emotional blocking apparently had begun in childhood in an unconscious effort to cope with the physical and sexual abuse she had endured from her stepfather. Lynn had been in therapy earlier to deal with issues related to her abuse, yet talking therapy had not revealed the tightly controlled and denied emotions that helped to perpetuate her stressful physical symptoms. EMT dissolved the surface stress so that she could examine the reasons why she feared examining her emotions.

Over the course of several visits, Lynn felt much more relaxed and comfortable with herself. She was much more aware of her physical tension and how it was related to particular stresses in her life, especially her relationship with her mother.

A year later, after the wedding, Lynn called me to report, as predicted, that her mother had made several loud and inappropriate remarks at the wedding. But Lynn had been fully prepared. She had reminded herself that her immediate and extended family already knew her mother well enough to expect such outbursts. And Lynn just told herself: "She can say what she wants. I can't control her."

Note: Lynn's EMT therapy would have been a more complicated matter if she had not already begun the difficult task of dealing with her history of sexual and physical abuse. If you have a history of traumatic experiences or current symptoms of post-traumatic stress disorder (disturbing memories of past events, flashbacks, nightmares and sleep problems, panicky feelings, and/or nearly constant fear or tension), or if you have symptoms of hallucinations, serious mood swings, or suicidal thoughts, do not attempt to treat yourself with EMT. Seek out the help of a qualified mental health professional for help with your situation. This advice also applies if you have a diagnosis of dissociative personality disorder (multiple personality), schizophrenia, bipolar disorder (manic depression), or borderline personality disorder.

Generalized Worry About the Family

Angela, age sixty-six, was divorced for twenty years and had two grown children, a son, thirty-nine, who was happily married, and a daughter, forty-one, who was married to a verbally abusive husband. She agonized about her daughter, Rose, as well as her own ninety-one-year-old mother whom she cared for during daily visits to her home. Angela acknowledged that she was a worrywart. A single phone call with her mother, who complained about various medical problems, would trigger apprehensions that her mother would not survive the night. As a result, she could not sleep and her worry could last for a couple of days until her mother seemed to overcome her latest bout of symptom flare-ups.

Also disturbing to Angela was her daughter's abusive marital relationship. Rose's husband had recently threatened to kill her if she sought a divorce. Because Rose lived a thousand miles away, Angela had little influence over the situation. It was up to her daughter to protect herself however she could, e.g. involving the police and the courts.

I taught Angela standard relaxation techniques that eased her stress somewhat, but whenever she heard bad news from her mother or daughter, her worry escalated, and no amount of relaxation could diffuse it. As an alternative to conventional relaxation, I tried the EMT in session as she focused on a moderate level of worry about her mother. After the first series of taps, she remarked that her usual worry escaped her consciousness completely. Two more rounds of taps reduced the worry about her mother to a 0. We then repeated the procedure for worry about her daughter with an even quicker resolution of this worry. Because Angela was so accustomed to ubiquitous worry, she was amazed that she could feel virtually worry free. She was assigned the taps for home use.

Looking for Daddy's Approval

Jamie and her husband, a couple in their early thirties, were ecstatic when their doctor confirmed she was pregnant. Jamie had been abused by her first husband, but her current husband was quite the opposite: supportive, tolerant, and accepting. Several positive things had happened to her recently, including finding a temporary job that would help her fund renovations to her kitchen. She called up her father hoping that he would be happy for her, but he made several derogatory remarks about overspending her budget for the kitchen remodeling and taking a "stupid" job. Even at age thirty-one, Jamie was devastated by his harsh reaction. Later, she realized that her lifelong goal, to be treated as "Daddy's little girl" was still influencing her, despite her father's long history of criticism and rejection. The EMT began with Jamie focusing on her anger and hurt about her father's stinging remarks. This is an excerpt of the session.

Jamie: [EMT.] I feel a lot more relaxed. At first, I was focusing on the telephone call from my dad and how upset I was getting. Then I couldn't really focus on it; it was fading in and out. I definitely have calmed down a lot.

Therapist: Let's continue. Focus on what you are thinking now about your dad. [EMT.] What's happening now?

Jamie: The stress feels like it's gone, and so is my headache.

Therapist: You had a headache because of the stress?

Jamie: Yeah. It was a stress headache. But I feel very relaxed now. I want to be in control of the situation with my father. I feel more whole now, more of a person.

Therapist: Let's continue with that thought. [EMT.] What's happening now?

Jamie: My stress level is completely down to a 0. I feel good again.

Therapist: That was quick. How are you thinking now about your dad's belittling remarks toward you?

Jamie: That it's *his* own frustration and anger, not so much directed toward me. I want to keep it in that kind of focus. I'll be able to take what he says not so personally, because I know that I'm a good person. I feel very confident about what I am doing. I don't have to be perfect, but I am a good person.

Therapist: What if your father rejects the things that you've done and says they are not good?

Jamie: It makes me feel like a victim, like a criminal. That is something I should have explained before. I felt like a criminal. That's how bad I felt. I guess I'll always analyze what he says. I'm not going to say, "Well, he doesn't know what he is talking about." I respect some of the things that he says, but I'm not going to accept his word as what I have to do. I want to live my own life.

Therapist: He always has found a way to criticize you. How do you feel about it right now?

Jamie: More accepting. That is him, and I have to accept him for who he is. He'll always do that to me.

Therapist: What if you tell him about good things that happen to you sometime in the future?

Jamie: He's going to find a way to play the devil's advocate, which he always does.

Therapist: When you call him up to tell him some good news, what are you going to expect to hear?

Jamie: I'm *not* going to call him up to tell him anymore. I'm not going to expect to hear what I feel I should hear.

Therapist:	He's not going to be a Robert Young from *Father Knows Best* when you call him?
Jamie:	No.
Therapist:	He's not going to be a Dr. Stone from *Donna Reed* either?
Jamie:	No.

This visit revealed that Jamie could still be hurt by her father's rejection of her decisions, but that she no longer had to devalue herself because of it. The EMT helped her to feel confident about her new temporary job and the planned kitchen renovations. In the past, she might have reconsidered her actions on the basis of her father's criticism. This time, she did not. Interestingly, her anger toward her father *did* return, but this could be viewed as healthy. She gave herself the *right* to feel and express anger about her father. This outcome is consistent with the EMT principle that the reprocessing of thoughts and feelings will progress to a constructive resolution. The anger surfaced because it was important to feel that emotion and be tolerant of it. With the EMT technique, her self-assurance showed substantial improvements over a two-week period. You would rarely see such rapid changes in standard psychotherapy.

EMT for Children's Problems

Young children who have stress-related problems can benefit from the EMT technique. Even with their limited verbal and cognitive skills, they can usually describe to some extent what is troubling them. Below is a session for Jimmy, age six, who attended kindergarten. His parents were concerned about his fear of going to sleep. Often his mother would stay in his bedroom to calm him at night. Jimmy was afraid of a bear or a monster attacking him while he slept.

Therapist:	Close your eyes and think about a monster attacking you in your sleep. That's pretty scary. Here we go. [EMT.] What's happening now?
Jimmy:	The monster ran away.
Therapist:	Do you feel more scared, less scared, or the same?
Jimmy:	Less scared.

Therapist:	Let your eyes close again. Think about the monster coming back. Here we go. [EMT.] Open your eyes. What's happening now?
Jimmy:	I'm starting to get less scared.
Therapist:	Good. Let's continue. Let your eyes close. [EMT.] Let your eyes open, and what's happening now?
Jimmy:	Well, the monster is looking at me. It might get me.
Therapist:	You mean to trample you or something?
Jimmy:	Yeah.
Therapist:	Okay. What do you think you could do about it?
Jimmy:	I would try to hit it with a slingshot.
Therapist:	All right. That's one way to go. Let's try that. Think of that. Let your eyes close. [EMT.] What's happening now?
Jimmy:	I got a few slingshots out at the monster.
Therapist:	Very good. More scared, less scared, or the same?
Jimmy:	Less scared. Each time I get less scared.
Therapist:	Think about the slingshots getting the monster. [EMT.] Eyes open, and what's happening now?
Jimmy:	Once the monster saw the slingshots, it ran away.
Therapist:	Do you still feel some fear though?
Jimmy:	Yeah, just a little.
Therapist:	Okay. Are you feeling relaxed?
Jimmy:	Yeah.
Therapist:	Let's see if we can get rid of the fear completely, so you don't even have a little bit left. Do you want to do that?
Jimmy:	Yeah.
Therapist:	Okay. Continue thinking about the monster and how you are going to defend yourself and all of that. [EMT.] Eyes open, and what's happening now?
Jimmy:	I feel much better.
Therapist:	How else could you scare off the monster?

Jimmy: Well, I would want to try screaming at it.

Therapist: Why don't we try that. Think of screaming at the monster, and it will run. [EMT.] Eyes open, and what's happening now?

Jimmy: My fear is totally, completely away. And the monster ran away after I screamed.

Therapist: Very good. No fear at all?

Jimmy: No.

Therapist: Boy, you did really good here, huh?

Jimmy was given further EMT to desensitize fears of having a nightmare about a creature that was half-man, half-dog that would attack him. During the EMT, he imagined killing the creature in a variety of ways including shooting, stabbing, and stomping it. His fear diminished from a high level to nothing, and that night he slept by himself. During the previous night, he needed his mother to sleep in the bed with him and was afraid to close his eyes until three o'clock in the morning. Several months later, he learned to do the tap procedure to himself so that he could relax and fall asleep without fear.

CHAPTER 12

Rapid
Relaxation and
Better Sleep

I f you are frequently tense, you may think, "I'm just too uptight to relax by any means." And perhaps this is true, because it does take time and attention to do standard relaxation techniques and achieve a good result. EMT is different: it produces relaxation more quickly than conventional relaxation techniques. In this chapter, I will show you how to combine EMT with standard relaxation techniques so you can relax and refresh yourself in only a few minutes time with almost no effort. Once you've learned to relax, you'll discover it has a number of benefits: (1) a sense of well-being and calm; (2) an improved ability to cope with stress; (3) improved physical and emotional health; (4) a greater ability to think clearly and organize your thoughts; and (5) improved sleep. If you are unable to conquer your stress problem with standard EMT, relaxation EMT may still be successful for you. Even if you are convinced that you can't relax, try the techniques below and you will probably feel calmer.

Breathing Focus

Breathing focus combines EMT with a phrase that you say to yourself in sync with your breathing. Sit in a comfortable chair in a quiet setting before eating. (After eating, digestion interferes with the process of deep relaxation.) Then think to yourself a long *reee* as you inhale and a slow *laaax* as you exhale. For the next minute, think to yourself the *relax* phrase until you are comfortable with it. Now, place your hands on your thighs and start tapping with your index fingers: left index finger taps left thigh once, right index finger taps right thigh once. Establish a left to right rhythm, about two taps per second. Continue the taps for three to four minutes. The combination of the taps and the *relax* phrase will produce a substantial release of stress and tension, and generate a pleasant feeling. If you wish to deepen the relaxation, continue the taps and the *relax* phrase for another two to three minutes. Your relaxed feeling may last for several hours or even the rest of the day. If you find it difficult to use the *relax* phrase, you can focus on your breathing alone without thinking any particular thought and achieve the same result.

As a way to relieve stress, I believe there is no technique that is quicker or more effective than EMT relaxation. Use the technique whenever you wish to banish stress, or simply to improve your sense of well-being and happiness.

Visualization with EMT

If you have a favorite relaxation image, such as a beach scene, a country setting, or a mountain resort, think of that particular image as you do the finger taps to your knees. You will find that the taps deepen the relaxation experience associated with the image you create.

An individual that I saw for chronic pain thought of enjoying the beach in Hawaii while she tapped her knees. In five minutes time, she was completely immersed in the image and reported that her experience, thinking about the beach scene, was more pleasurable and calming with the EMT taps. The sample beach scene below can help you fill in those pleasant details if you wish to use the beach image.

> Imagine yourself spending an afternoon at the beach. The sand feels warm and soft against your skin. You are sitting on the sand observing the ocean, the azure blue water; viewing the flow of the waves as they move rhythmically to the shore, the water becoming a light transparent green as it flows to the shoreline. And you see the whitecaps on the waves as the waves roll onto the shore; yes, waves gently reaching the shore, like sparkling water spilling on the sand; feeling a salty, refreshing spray in the air, that refreshing misty spray permeating your body—so wonderfully invigorating and uplifting; revitalizing and relaxing.
>
> Allow yourself the next few moments to imagine the pleasant flow of the waves onto the shore as they rise and fall, rise and fall. Go ahead now and imagine the waves. *(Pause for about five seconds.)*
>
> All right. Very good. Now you decide to take an easy stroll along the beach as you view the surf; yes, observe the curving shoreline off in the distance, the curving shoreline as it merges with the horizon. As you walk onward, onward, you feel the sand crunching beneath your feet; such a pleasant sensation—the warm crunchy sand. It complements the warmth of the sun overhead. Feel the warmth of the sun on your back, that gentle warmth flowing down your back and throughout your body; comfortable warmth from the sun filling you with pleasant sensations. With your senses so very aware, you notice the sand dunes rising along the beach, sand dunes with isolated clumps of tall grass on their slopes. Noticing

the tall grass gently swaying in the breeze. The breezes creating tranquil feelings.

And as you walk onward, you hear the sound of sea-gulls in the distance. A flock of white seagulls approaching, flying so easily, gliding in the wind, making their distinctive sounds passing overhead. Now flying off in the distance, leaving you with a feeling of serenity. . . . Now feeling a gentle breeze at your back. The gentle breeze coaxing you further along, heightening your senses.

As you look across the waves, you see a sleek white sailboat moving through the water—the boat moving so gracefully, the sails filled with gently sweeping winds. Enjoy the silent steadiness of the boat as it moves along with the wind.

Now as you gaze further toward the horizon, you see the sun setting. Yes, the sun setting in a full display of vivid colors: bright yellows, deep reds, and burnt oranges against the light gray clouds and a pale blue sky. As the sun descends, it projects a long wedge of yellow light across the water; slowly sinking down. And a breathtaking serenity begins to pervade the atmosphere. An emerging serenity so deep that it is fully absorbing your senses.

Now you begin to conclude the experience—finish the experience with acceptance and peace, acceptance and peace. . . . Allow yourself the next minute, all the time in the world, all the time you need to bring yourself back to wakefulness, your eyes opening slowly, feeling relaxed and refreshed. (Friedberg 1995, 58-59)

EMT Relaxation as a Sleep Technique

Nearly one out of two Americans has trouble with their sleep. Sleep problems can take many forms: trouble falling asleep, staying asleep, frequent awakenings during the night, waking up too early in the morning, or simply feeling unrefreshed after a full night's sleep. Often there is a stress factor in sleep disturbances. If you have problems falling asleep, you may lie awake worrying specifically about not falling asleep. For example, your thinking might be, "What if I can't sleep tonight? How will I function tomorrow?" Or you may be frustrated about not sleeping as well as you would like to, thinking as you lie awake, "I can't stand this sleep problem!"

Of course, worrying about our sleeplessness isn't the only stress that keeps us awake at night. A second type of stress involves focusing on worry, frustration, annoyance, or anger about any other specific problem, aside from our sleeplessness.

Dwelling on negative emotions or catastrophizing about a difficult situation will ensure a restless night. A third cause of sleep difficulties is thinking pleasant, exciting thoughts while at the same time trying to fall asleep. Exciting thoughts will uplift you but are clearly incompatible with the feeling of relaxation that induces sleepiness and a good night's rest. In addition to such psychologically generated stress, there are a number of medical problems and symptoms that contribute to sleep disturbance, including chronic pain and chronic fatigue.

How can EMT help with sleep? If you have trouble falling asleep, I recommend that you focus on the *relax* phrase while lying in bed, and at the same time, tap your thighs with your index fingers, left index finger to left thigh, right index finger to right thigh (see chapter 6). Repeat this left to right motion while focusing on the *relax* phrase and you will, in a few minutes, feel dreamy and relaxed. Continue the taps until you are immersed in this feeling of serenity (about five minutes), then stop the taps. Continue thinking the *relax* phrase until you doze off to sleep. Use the same technique if you wake up during the middle of the night and can't fall back to sleep, or if you awaken too early.

You'll see results with this technique the first time you try it for any sleep problem. There is no need for extended practice as might be required for a standard relaxation procedure. The EMT produces a completely automatic relaxation response. EMT at bedtime accomplishes two things: It distracts you from stressful thoughts, and it brings about the physical and mental relaxation that induces restful sleep.

If stressful thoughts and feelings prevent the relaxation EMT from easing you into sleep, try this alternative: Deliberately focus on your stressful feelings and thoughts and do the EMT taps while in bed, until the stress is completely gone. With the stress-focusing technique, you are likely to resolve at least some of the issues behind your worry, anger, frustration, or other distressing emotion. You have then overcome your stress problem and your sleep difficulty with a single EMT. What could be more efficient?

The following is a personal example of how I used EMT to improve and lengthen my sleep:

I was waking up much earlier than I wanted to almost every night for several weeks. I would go to sleep at 11:00 P.M. and wake up at 5:00 A.M. and not be able to return to sleep. To feel rested, I do need eight hours of sleep. Although I could function on the six hours, my fatigue would accumulate over time until I would collapse one night and sleep for ten or eleven hours.

By accident, I discovered how the EMT could work to improve and lengthen my sleep. When I woke up one morning at 5:00 A.M., I noticed that I was dwelling on one thought: "I hate waking up early! I hate waking up early!" Perhaps this belief was creating frustration and preoccupation with my sleep problem. I focused on that thought while doing the EMT taps. The thought dissipated until it entirely faded away, and I fell back to sleep.

The next day, even though I was somewhat tired, I did not dwell on my loss of sleep or how it was affecting me, something that I now realize I had been doing. The next night, I woke up early as usual, but fell back to sleep within fifteen to twenty minutes, something I had not been able to do previously. I realized that my persistent frustration about early awakening prevented my falling back to sleep. The simple EMT intervention made me more tolerant of my sleep problem and allowed me to return to sleep rather than focusing on my frustration.

If you have a sleep problem, use the EMT method to focus on relaxation or to alleviate stressful thoughts, such as I did, until you experience deepening feelings of calm. You will have a more restful night's sleep.

CHAPTER 13

The Range of EMT Applications: From Simple Stress Reduction to Life Reassessment

Stress Reduction in Everyday Life

Our personal stress levels will peak from time to time as hassles and frustrations build at work, home, or elsewhere. When problems and conflicts do not yield to any immediate or obvious solution, the next logical step might involve talking to a spouse, a friend, or a coworker. You may receive important psychological support from these sources, but you may not feel true *relief*. When stress becomes unmanageable or overwhelming, I have found EMT to be the most powerful means to alleviate it without the use of medications. When you feel overwhelmed, the most important and immediate goal should be a reduction in distress. EMT does two important things in this situation: It provides a powerful diversion from upsets—a welcome shift from persistent feelings of distress. It also creates a potent level of relaxation and comfort with minimal effort. There can be no more powerful intervention than one that rapidly interrupts high intensity aggravation. Once the diversion and relaxation effects of EMT are in place, then you can contemplate your problems with a greater sense of proportion, understanding, and even optimism.

On a personal level, I use EMT when I am having heated arguments with someone close to me. Even in the middle of an argument, I can discreetly tap my knees and then feel my shoulders loosen and my feelings of anger and frustration diminish. As a result, I feel less blaming toward the other person and better able to express my thoughts without rancor. When I use this simple self-control technique, it leads to a better resolution of the conflict.

Life Reassessment With EMT

Our inner strengths and deepest aspirations may be obscured or even thwarted by ongoing stress in our lives. I believe that once the disruptive influences of stress are minimized, you can identify the underlying positive forces and integrate them into your daily life. EMT facilitates this process. As your feelings of conflict, distress, and turmoil are released, EMT frees you to define important directions in your life, directions that are not simply a function of conforming to what others expect or reaching goals that no longer have meaning for you.

In one sense, EMT helps to address the imbalances in our lives. Often we are pulled by motivations that lead us to overwork or to over focus on a particular problem, and at the same time, we neglect our inner needs and desires. Once EMT clears away the conscious stress, we become more aware of the unhealthy imbalances in our life. Then we can redirect ourselves and nurture our often neglected inner selves. The opportunities for rebalancing that are revealed by EMT are unique for each individual. In our work focused culture, it may mean a de-emphasis of work and a rededication to family, relationships, and spirituality. Or our changed attitudes may dissolve our fears and open us to establishing new life goals. We may find ourselves taking a new look at the value of contemplative leisure time rather than "playing hard."

Transforming Priorities

A close friend of mine, Alan, a single man of forty-eight, was quite successful in his career as a financial analyst. Yet he rejected the possibility of a family because he did not have an interest in kids. He was so driven by his work and leisure time sports that he rarely examined the nagging feelings of dissatisfaction that emerged in his unguarded moments. Although he did not believe he had a problem, I used the EMT on him as a simple experiment to see where it would lead. I had him focus on the dissatisfied feeling while I did the EMT taps. He began to get images of a long time woman friend who had just adopted a baby and became a single mother. He still saw his friend occasionally along with her adopted little girl, and began to recognize a growing attachment to the toddler. It was difficult for him to acknowledge these feelings, because he had discounted the possibility of having children. Although he had thought that he simply didn't have an interest in children, the EMT focused his attention on the juxtaposition of this lifelong belief and the emerging reality that he was becoming closer to this child. Perhaps his desire for a family was hidden, denied, or repressed. Clearly it was there, and the EMT procedure uncovered it or, at the very least, highlighted an ongoing evolution in his thoughts and feelings about this child.

Alan began to recognize the importance of this relationship to him and remarked that his friendship with the girl's mother had become stronger since the adoption. This was an illuminating new insight for him. Over the next several months he became closer still to the child, and the relationship with the mother improved. He began to feel that his life now had a satisfying symmetry between his intellectually driven work and the warm, loving environment with this child and her mother. The EMT facilitated this inner awareness and seemed to coax and encourage it to develop more fully.

A second example of major life changes facilitated through EMT illustrates another type of transformation. At age fifty-seven, David had worked as a safety engineer at a federally funded biological laboratory. For the past fifteen years, he had insured the safety of personnel working at the facility. He enjoyed the challenges and the responsibilities of his position. However, he was plagued by uninvolved upper management, who often hired marginally competent people to perform sensitive, highly skilled jobs. David had to monitor their job performance to insure adequate safety precautions were followed.

Although he had written a training manual for safety drills and numerous other essential procedures for the laboratory, the manual's recommendations were seldom followed and potential hazards often arose. At one point, some of the more egregious problems at the lab were reported by a local newspaper. Despite the negative publicity, little changed to improve safety conditions. David was increasingly frustrated and angry at the indifference of management and the poor cooperation among his coworkers.

Ultimately, he became depressed about the seemingly insurmountable problems at his job. He suffered from high blood pressure and stomach ulcers as well. As the medical and psychological problems grew more severe, he took a medical leave from his job and underwent treatment with antidepressants drugs and medications for high blood pressure and ulcers. During the first few therapy sessions, I was unable to relieve either his anger about the lab or his severely depressed mood. Then I tried a series of EMT tap procedures, all of which worked to some degree to reduce his emotional stress and even boost his mood. But the final procedure produced a breakthrough of sorts.

In response to the final set of EMT taps, David realized he wasn't a failure because he couldn't cope with the current difficulties of his job. And he began to look at his career in a more objective way. His many successes had advanced the mission of the lab by insuring that safety procedures were followed. David began to feel satisfied with what he had accomplished, despite the aggravations and setbacks. Following EMT, his attitude about leisure changed as well. He again enjoyed the simple pleasures of eating, walking with his dog, and communicating with friends across the country. I believe that the EMT tap procedures helped him to turn this important corner. Once he rediscovered pleasure in his life, the therapy and medication began to work much more effectively.

During the several months of his medical leave, David reevaluated his position at the lab. His job satisfaction was outweighed by uncontrollable personnel factors that prevented him from doing his job properly. The stress created by this conflict had taken a toll on his health and well-being. Rather than resume his struggle at the lab and compromise his health further, he decided to take an early retirement package and move to the South. He had a number of other skills, such as carpentry and musical ability, that would allow him to sustain a modest but satisfying lifestyle.

I spoke to David after he moved. He no longer needed the lab to feel competent and worthy. Without that self-imposed pressure, David was able to enjoy his new life. Significantly, his depression lifted, his stress-related medical conditions eased, and, as a result, he required less medication.

So beyond the immediate stress reduction aspects of EMT, you can proceed to a deeper, perhaps more spiritual, exploration with the procedure and gain a greater understanding of your life priorities. Ask yourself during the EMT, "Are my current priorities working for me? Do they produce the satisfactions that I need?" If there is a feeling of discontent generated by thinking about your life goals and directions, are you willing to examine the reasons behind the dissatisfaction? When the reasons are discovered, are you willing to experiment with new activities or to at least focus on previously devalued activities that may now, in fact, be more important to you? The EMT will facilitate the redirection of your thinking toward what is important to you, even if you do not realize its importance at the moment. Then you can choose to experiment with these new directions, and you may ultimately find a deeper, more sustained sense of fulfillment.

References

Cassidy, A. 1996. What pushes your stress button? *Working Mother*, July, 18–22.

Cioffi, D. 1991. Beyond attentional strategies: cognitive-perceptual model of somatic interpretation. *Psychological Bulletin* 109:25–41.

Ellis, A. 1973. *A Guide to Rational Living*. North Hollywood: Wilshire Book Company.

Fawzy, F. I., et al. 1993. Malignant melanoma. Effects of an early structured psychiatric intervention, coping, and affective state on recurrence and survival 6 years later. *Archives of General Psychiatry* 50:681–689.

Friedberg, F., and L. A. Jason. 2001. Chronic fatigue syndrome and fibromyalgia. Clinical assessment and treatment. *Journal of Clinical Psychology.* In press.

Friedberg, F. 1995. *Coping with Chronic Fatigue Syndrome. Nine Things You Can Do.* Oakland, Calif.: New Harbinger.

Friedman, M., C. E. Thoresen, J. J. Gill, et al. 1986. Alteration of Type A behavior and its effect on cardiac recurrence. Summary results of the coronary results of the recurrent coronary prevention project. *American Heart Journal* 112:653–665.

Knipe, J. 1997 Identifying hidden blocking beliefs. *EMDRIA Newsletter* 2:10–11.

Krantz, D. S., W. J. Kop, H. T. Santiago, and J. S. Gottdiener. 1996. Mental stress as a trigger of myocardial ischemia and infarction. *Cardiology Clinics* 14:271–287.

Luecken, L. J., et al. 1997. Stress in employed women: impact of marital status and children at home on neurohormone output and home strain. *Psychosomatic Medicine* 59:352–359.

Marquis, J. 1991. A report on seventy-eight cases treated by eye movement desensitization. *Journal of Behavior Therapy and Experimental Psychiatry* 22(3):187–192.

Reich, R. 2001. *The Future of Success.* New York: Knopf.

Rozanski, A., J. A. Blumenthal, and J. Kaplan. 1999. Impact of psychological factors on the pathogenesis of cardiovascular disease and implications for therapy. *Circulation* 99:2192–2197.

Sarno, J. E. 1998. *The Mind-Body Prescription. Healing the Body, Healing the Pain.* New York: Warner Books.

Schor, J. 1991. *The Overworked American: The Unexpected Decline of Leisure.* New York: Basic Books.

Shapiro, F. 1995. *Eye Movement Desensitization and Reprocessing. Basic Principles, Protocols, and Procedures.* New York: Guilford.

Smyth, L. 1994. *Overcoming Post-traumatic Stress Disorder.* Oakland, Calif.: New Harbinger Publications.

Spiegel, D., J. R. Bloom, H. C. Kraemer, and E. Gottheil. 1989. Effect of psychosocial treatment on survival of patients with metatastic breast cancer. *Lancet* 2(8668) 888–891.

Walsh, M. W. 2000. As hot economy pushes up overtime, fatigue becomes a labor issue. *New York Times,* September, 17.

Weekes, C. 1969. *Hope and Help for Your Nerves.* Toronto: Bantam.

Williams, R. B., and P. W. Williams. 1994. *Anger Kills: Seventeen Strategies for Controlling the Hostility That Can Harm Your Health.* New York: Harperperennial Library.

Wirsching, M., H. Stierlin, F. Hoffmann, G. Weber, and B. Wirsching. 1982. Psychological identification of breast cancer patients before biopsy. *Journal of Psychosomatic Research* 26:1–10.

Wolpe, J., and J. Abrams. 1991. Postraumatic stress disorder overcome by eye-movement desensitization. *Journal of Behavior Therapy and Experimental Psychiatry* 22(1):39–43.

Fred Friedberg, Ph.D., has been a clinical psychologist in private practice for 20 years. He is also a clinical assistant professor in the Department of Psychiatry, School of Medicine at the State University of New York at Stony Brook. Friedberg is the author of the popular book *Coping with Chronic Fatigue Syndrome: Nine Things You Can Do*. His work has been published in the *Journal of Clinical Psychology, American Psychologist, Professional Psychology: Research and Practice*, and other journals. In addition, he has conducted professional workshops for the American Psychological Association, the Association for the Advancement of Behavior Therapy, and the Society of Behavioral Medicine. Friedberg lives in Cornwall, CT.

Some Other
New Harbinger Titles

The Trigger Point Therapy Workbook, Item TPTW $19.95

Fibromyalgia and Chronic Myofascial Pain Syndrome, Item FMS $19.95

Kill the Craving, Item KC $18.95

Rosacea, Item ROSA $13.95

Thinking Pregnant, Item TKPG $13.95

Shy Bladder Syndrome, Item SBDS $13.95

Help for Hairpullers, Item HFHP $13.95

Coping with Chronic Fatigue Syndrome, Item CFS $13.95

The Stop Smoking Workbook, Item SMOK $17.95

Multiple Chemical Sensitivity, Item MCS $16.95

Breaking the Bonds of Irritable Bowel Syndrome, Item IBS $14.95

Parkinson's Disease and the Art of Moving, Item PARK $15.95

The Addiction Workbook, Item AWB $17.95

The Interstitial Cystitis Survival Guide, Item ICS $14.95

Illness and the Art of Creative Self-Expression, Item EXPR $13.95

Don't Leave it to Chance, Item GMBL $13.95

The Chronic Pain Control Workbook, 2nd edition, Item PN2 $18.95

Perimenopause, 2nd edition, Item PER2 $16.95

The Family Recovery Guide, Item FAMG $15.95

Healthy Baby, Toxic World, Item BABY $15.95

I'll Take Care of You, Item CARE $12.95

Call **toll free, 1-800-748-6273,** or log on to our online bookstore at **www.newharbinger.com** to order. Have your Visa or Mastercard number ready. Or send a check for the titles you want to New Harbinger Publications, Inc., 5674 Shattuck Ave., Oakland, CA 94609. Include $4.50 for the first book and 75¢ for each additional book, to cover shipping and handling. (California residents please include appropriate sales tax.) Allow two to five weeks for delivery.

Prices subject to change without notice.